THE BATTLE RAGES ON...

A PANORAMIC LOOK AT SPIRITUAL REALITIES AND SPIRITUAL WARFARE FROM BEFORE TIME BEGAN

DR. GERALD D. ROBISON

Published by Leadership Books, Inc. Las Vegas, NV – New York, NY

www. LeadershipBooks.com

Hardcover: 978-1-965401-61-3
Paperback: 978-1-965401-21-7
Workbook: 978-1-965401-22-4
eBook: 978-1-965401-23-1

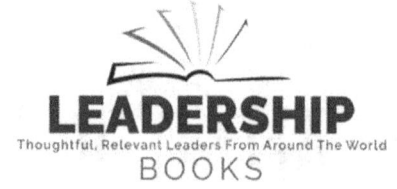

LEADERSHIP
Thoughtful, Relevant Leaders From Around The World
BOOKS

Author's Note:

If a Bible translation is listed, the quote is as written in that translated version of Scripture. If there is no translation mentioned, it is my paraphrase of the Bible verse or just a reference for where you can find further reading on the subject matter. This was done for flow in this format of Jesus and Adam sending letters back and forth

Dedication

This book is dedicated to Dr Michael Heiser, the man who opened my mind and my heart to understand the deeper, forgotten and overlooked things of God. He helped me to see and understand the Unseen Realm.

Endorsements

"I have been blessed for several years by the bible teaching of Dr. Gerald Robison. In this book, he presents us with a unique approach to scriptures that may seem difficult. But his methodology encourages us to not look away from those hard passages but instead to read for the first time."

Buck Burch

Missions Catalyst, Georgia Baptist Mission Board

"I am honored to endorse Gerald Robison and his new book on Spiritual Warfare. Gerald is a faithful Bible scholar whose teaching is firmly grounded in the truth of God's Word. With clarity and conviction, he exposes the schemes of the enemy while magnifying the power of Christ's victory. This book is both biblically sound and spiritually practical, offering guidance for believers who desire to stand strong in the Lord. I highly commend Gerald Robison and this timely resource to all who long to live in triumph through Christ."

Darey Kittle

Senior Pastor at Salem Baptist Church in Dalton, GA

"I have known Gerald Robison for over 25 years. His heart belongs to the Lord ...along with his mind. He's using it to help the body of Christ see what they can't see: there is a spiritual battle raging around us that we are completely unaware of. Don't go through life unaware of the battle you are in."

Bob Sjogren

President/Co-Founder of UnveilinGLORY

"In The Battle Rages On… Gerald Robison pulls back the curtain on the spiritual realm with clarity, conviction, and deep Biblical insight. He tackles the hard questions many believers wrestle with, about evil, suffering, and spiritual warfare, with both theological depth and pastoral compassion. I have deep admiration and respect for Gerald—not only as a strong Biblical teacher, but as a true mentor and spiritual father to many, including myself. His ability to combine solid theology with real-world wisdom and a disarming sense of humor makes this book both engaging and impactful. I believe it will awaken readers to the reality of the unseen battle and equip them to stand firm in faith."

Miles Phelps

Director of "City For the Nations"

For over 30 years I have seen how Gerald teaches the Word of God with passion and creative skill. I have discovered game changing perspectives listening to him on many subjects and as an author he will take you on a journey to rethink and discover the Scriptures anew.Martin Deacon

President

Teach Every Nation

Table of Contents

Preface

Once my eyes were opened to seeing the unseen world that surrounds us all, they couldn't be closed again. I began a journey into a realm I knew little about—but grew to love.

I hope it does the same for you, dear reader.

Introduction

Three small words make one of the most famous lines given to all humanity. The Bible begins with them: "In the beginning..." Those three words are followed by seven more that complete the thought: "...God created the heavens and the earth."

Together, those are among the most famously recognized words throughout the history of mankind, and they set the stage for the world's most historic and intricate story of how we, life itself and the cosmos began.

But do these words give us the true beginning... or just the start of what we need to know about ourselves, our world, our past and our future?

There is so much conflicting and confusing information everywhere we look. How do you know what to believe?

Have you ever wondered:

- Is spiritual warfare real?
- Does the Devil really have armies of spiritual beings that hate us and want to drag us to hell?
- If my pastor says one thing, a popular book says another, a podcast says something else entirely–how do I know what's really *true*?
- How can I deepen my spiritual understanding beyond what is just on the surface?

These are only a few of the myriads of questions that perplex modern readers and inquirers of the Bible when it comes to exploring and understanding the spiritual realm.

And they are just a few of the questions I have to put before God myself. Like you, I seek answers... not opinions, not doctrinal bullet-points, and not denominational thoughts. I want answers—REAL answers. I know you do too. You might think I'd have them by now. After all:

- I've been a Bible student and minister all my life.
- I pastored churches on three continents.
- I taught at a Bible college and a seminary.
- I've earned four graduate degrees in ministry, psychology, counseling, education, and theology.
- I've trained Bible teachers across 25 nations, worked with mission organizations, and more.

Yet, I still have questions.

I wish I could stand before God and ask these questions—but, to see God and live, it's impossible. Were I able to stand in the radiance of His magnificence with His vivacity penetrating my being and his illuminating, iridescent glory overwhelming me, it would disassemble me piece by piece, cell by cell, microbe by microbe. I would become similar to how the prophet Isaiah described himself upon seeing God:

> "Woe is me, I am undone and ruined, for my eyes
> have seen the King, the Lord of hosts."
> —*Isaiah 6:5 (AMPC)*

I dream of a time before created worlds, prior to seraphim and cherubim singing at the throne of God in heaven. I imagine me seeing Him before the first words of creation were vocalized, picturing myself standing and watching from a place where God was, which was really no place back then because all that existed was the Father, Son, and Holy Spirit, an eternal Trinity in all its glory, adorned with the brilliance of God's being.

Describing that picture would be too wondrous and wholly inadequate for words—inexpressible. How is it possible to utter the unutterable? It's not! Helpful words would be too weak, small and frustrating to leave my lips. Descriptors like powerful, overwhelming, intense, and tremendous would fail to adequately communicate the awe and wonder of His being. I'm sure this unimaginable brilliance is what Jesus was referring to when he said:

> "And now, Father, glorify me in your own presence, with the glory that I had with you before the world existed."
>
> —*John 17:5 (ESV)*

But, oh, if I could just be alone with the spiritually physical God, seeing Him right in front of me, being able to ask the questions that have befuddled my mind and ransacked my understanding, questions for which mankind has sought answers for ages. Yet, getting where He is visually present is impossible for me right now. What am I to do? I can only search, exploring the words, mind, and heart of Christ, allowing Him to guide me to answers sprinkled throughout the Bible.

As the next best thing to sitting with God in our living rooms or on a park bench, personally posing questions to Him while in His presence, I'll present the questions you and I might ask. God's Word will provide His answers: Jesus is the Living Word, and Scripture is His written Word. Both are the Word of God and they supply the answers and insights to our hearts and minds.

To ask my questions and maybe yours, too, I'll borrow the name of the original human created by God, Adam. But not the original Adam. This book's questioner is a 21st-century Adam whose name is taken from our oldest relative. And why not use the name of Adam? If the first person had the honor and privilege of walking and talking with God in the midst of His garden, inquiring all he wanted of God, why not employ Adam's namesake to ask Jesus about life's continuing mysteries?

Each of these imagined letters begin with our modern Adam inquiring of Jesus, who then responds with explanations offered in the Bible.

In this book you will find the truth—the reasonable answers to the lingering questions so many of us have about the spiritual realm and spiritual warfare.

And, thus we begin.

1

Before the Beginning

Dear Jesus,

Well, I've been at it again–listening to radio preachers, Christian TV personalities, my pastor, my group leader, convention and conference teachers, and more as they open the floodgates to teach about the spiritual realm and spiritual warfare.

I know they want the best for their listeners and viewers, and each thinks they are *rightly dividing* (accurately handling) *the Word*, but they seem so contradictory in their outlooks, each one emphasizing something different, and I know they can't all be right.

Technology has advanced to such a degree that listeners and viewers are inundated with a mishmash of information and it's hard to know who to believe, who to follow and who to learn from. Many of them seemingly remind me of *concrete*–that is, they are thoroughly mixed up and permanently set!

Now, I don't mind being permanently set, in fact, I prefer it but I want to be set with reasonable, Scriptural answers to my lingering questions about the spiritual realm and spiritual warfare.

That's why I wanted to come directly to the source and ask you about these things. Angels, devils, demons, principalities, powers, rulers of wickedness, powers in the air—is any of this stuff real? Why are we here? Why did you even make us? What are your plans and hopes for us as people?

If you're God, and you're good, and you're omnipotent, why is there evil in the world? Is the opposite of God the Devil? Is there *really* a Devil? Does he really have armies of spiritual beings that hate us and want to drag us to hell?

Is there *really* a battle going on between Evil and Good? How much sway and influence does evil have in this world? Will Good win in the end? How do we know that?

Is there life after death? Is there really a Heaven? How about Hell? Is paradise and heaven the same thing? Are the Lake of Fire and hell the same? Does Satan really rule in hell? Is there even a real character called Satan?

People talk about spiritual warfare, but I've never seen an angel or a demon. So, how can that be real? And if it is real, how do they actually affect us? Do we really need to worry? I mean, if spirits don't have bodies, how can they interfere with our lives?

If heaven is real, is it true that there is only one way to get there? What about all the other religions in the world? Can they all be wrong? Can more than one be right? What am I to think about the other gods? Are you the only one? And, if so, who are these others? Are they real? And if so, why do some consider you the only god?

As you can see, I've got questions.
I'm confused.
I need answers and clarity.
Can you help me understand?
Yours truly,

–Adam

Dear Adam,

You do have a lot of questions, and I'm delighted to help you understand the world I created, why I put you in it, and how it all came to be the way it is.

But, at the moment, you're all over the board. To give you adequate answers, we'll need to take this world of confusion you carry and take it one piece at a time.

I think if I tell you my story and tell it from the beginning, it will help put everything into some semblance of order and you'll gain a new perspective and see how all the pieces fit together. Then, when you see the big picture, you'll understand all that you asked–and more than you dared dream to ask.

First, if we're going to start at the beginning, you need to understand that when you read the words, "In the beginning...", that wasn't the real beginning. That is, it wasn't the *original* beginning. It was the beginning of you, your world, your cosmos... but it wasn't *My* beginning. There was a time before the beginning, there was a time before time began.

I was there... and I wasn't alone.

Sounds confusing? It might, but it doesn't have to be.

Everything you need to know and remember you'll find in My words, the words of the prophets, and those of the apostles.

Yes, the Bible does begin with the words, "In the beginning..." but you will find those same words elsewhere and it describes the beginning that was *before* that beginning. There was a time before there were stars, planets and a cosmos by which you even measure time.

In this *other* beginning, there was me... I was *with* God and I *was* God. There was God the Father and God the Son (as you know us). I was in the beginning with God. Adam, this was the beginning that was before what you think about, when you think about those three words, "In the beginning." As I said, I was in the beginning with God.

I was there before anything that was made was made. When it came time to make and create it, it was all done by me. All things that were made were made through me... and without me nothing was made! There was no place, no thing and no life without me. In me was life and I put it where and how I wanted it (John 1:1-4).

But, before I put life anywhere, there was just the Godhead, and an incomprehensible glory that radiated from us. What splendor and grandeur there was! Our glory, it was... well, it was splendidly luxurious, and I guess you could say it was *glorious*. And the grand scale of it all was inexpressible: it was ineffable! It's no wonder that when I came in bodily form that I always remembered and longed for that again. Do you remember when I prayed...

> "And now, Father, glorify me in your own presence
> with the glory I had with you before the world
> existed."
>
> *(John 17:5)*

That is what my prayer was all about. Oh, how I missed it!

Now before you start with all the "I wish I could have seen it" comments, let me assure you that you will. There will come a day, a time when I remake all things and you will see it for yourself. If you'll remember, I prodded the Apostle Paul with my thoughts about this. I told him,

> "What no eye has seen, nor ear heard, nor the heart
> of man imagined, that's what [I'm] preparing for those
> who love [Me]."
>
> *(1 Corinthians 2:9)*

I couldn't keep quiet about it. I even whispered it to the disciple I loved, John, and he passed it on for others to read. I told him about the city and the place of heaven to come. I hastened to remind him that it will be one of those *glorious* moments in time. I gave him a glimpse of it all when I told him about the city–the New Jerusalem–that will come down out of heaven. How that the city will have no need of the sun or the moon to shine on it, for the glory of God the Father, and we will give it its light and its lamp will be Me (Revelations 21:23-24).

I even recall telling my followers before I returned to my Father, that there were going to be many abiding places in my Father's realm, and that I was going to prepare a place for both them and *you*. In that way, wherever I was going to be, you could be there too. I want you to see it, to experience it, and I want you to walk there with me. I emphasized that this was a truth that could be trusted.

As I told my disciples, if this was not true, I wouldn't have said anything at all (John 14:1-3). This isn't something I made up! So, yes, you will get to see it all, when the time comes.

The time has not yet come - but it will – I assure you. And, it will have been worth the wait. But that's still in the future. Our current conversation is about the past, so let me get back to that and close this note by saying,

At that time, all was so glorious and we, the Godhead, had no needs. We were perfect in all our ways, just as we still are.

This missive should raise more questions for you to ponder and ask. For now, I'll look forward to your next inquiry.

Self-sustainingly yours,

—Jesus

PS–Do you see, in the *original* beginning, there was no enmity, no rebellion, no faults, no sin? It was just the harmony, unity, and the splendor of the Godhead... Me, My Father and the Holy Spirit. There is no battle and no raging... but it's on the horizon and it will come.

2

There's Nothing Gooder than God

Dear Jesus,

You were right.

As I read of the glory you held before there was anything and anyone else, I did find myself wishing I could have been there to see, hear, and experience the glory of your self-existence in eternity past. It's hard, really hard, to wait for you to bring everything to a state of completion and see the wonder of it all.

However, if you thought I'd have more questions, well, you're right. I mean, if you were self-sustaining, self-gratified and without needs, I have to ask, *Why would you bother to create anything at all?*

You didn't need to create us.

You didn't need a world to be brought into existence.

You didn't need people, animals, birds, fish grass, planets, or the cosmos.

So, *why?*

Why put yourself to so much bother?

Why create beings that could go so wrong?

Why make a place where sin could abound?

I can't wrap my head around this, so let this note be short and concise by just asking, "WHY?"

Questioningly yours,

—Adam

Dear Adam,

Well, it didn't take long for you to get right to the point. "Why?" is an excellent question and it deserves an equally excellent answer. But know this – an excellent answer requires rigorous thought. The answer won't be easy… but I think it will be satisfying.

You asked, if all was so glorious and God the Father, myself, and the Holy Spirit were content and satisfied and had no needs, why would I even consider creating and making anything at all?

- Just because I was creative didn't mean I *needed* to create. If that was true, I would still be creating.

- Just because we were alone, didn't mean I was lonely and *needed* to create company for myself.

- Just because I was loving, merciful, gracious, and patient, didn't mean I *needed* something to love, someone to extend mercy to or even give grace to. Those attributes merely describe my character–they don't point to something I need to exhibit.

There is no good answer that implies, in any shape or form, that I am in need, or that something else is needed to complete me.

So, let's go back to what you know and start down this path again:

- The Godhead is wholly satisfied
- The Godhead is completely self-sustaining
- The Godhead is without need
- It is omnipotent, omniscient, omnipresent
- I am loving, I am merciful, I am forgiving, I am gracious
- I am *good*

- I did not create out of any need – for there was none.

So, then, *why* would I create? Surely, there had to be some motivation to move me from self-satisfied to creating. It was not to fulfill some need lurking within me. No, no, no… I created because creation accomplishes something that I value and desire to sustain.

What values do I hold?

I value Goodness, Truth, Beauty, Justice, and more. These are my own attributes and I value them, I uphold them and I AM THEM. These attributes don't just describe me – they are me. They have their source in me. That is, without me, these do not exist.

Listen carefully to what I'm about to say, Adam…

I don't *need* anything, but I do *value* some things.

And those things are the very qualities and values that exist within me. And while this might sound self-centered, I'm going to say it anyway, I value me. It's not that I value these traits as something separate from me, they ARE me. They come from me. I define them.

- If you want to speak of the greatest good–you're speaking of me.

- If you want to speak of that which is true–you're going to speak of me.

- If you want to speak of that which is honest–you're going to speak of me.

- If you want to speak of that which is beautiful–you're going to speak of me.

I value me! Why? Because that is where the greatest values lie, they are within Me. Maybe this will help you to understand why I said I am a jealous God. If I wanted to give you that which is *best*, then I must give you myself! If I allowed you to consider anything, other than me, as that which is of ultimate and greatest worth, then I would not love you. Loving you means I want only the *best* for you. And the *best* for you is me.

Adam, there is nothing "gooder" than God. There is nothing gooder than me. Yes, I know, that's *terrible grammar*, but it's *great theology*!

Therefore, let me say this again… If I want to give you the very best, I must give you myself. Why? Because there are no values greater than those found within me.

You see, I have a *desire*, not a *need*, to promulgate that which is *good*. And I find that my creation is the best means to do that. By creating the universe, the cosmos, people, animals, birds, fish, spiritual beings, human beings, spiritual realms and earthly ones, I disseminate my glory, my values, and my goodness.

Adam, you might be familiar with the phrase, "love loves to love." That is, love enjoys perpetuating itself. It loves loving and wants love to grow and spread. In a similar way, Good loves to proclaim and perpetuate more goodness.

While you may not see it yet, creation will expand and increase the *good* value that is within me. This is why I encouraged the apostle Mark to write,

> "There is no one (essentially and perfectly, morally) good—except God alone."
> —*Mark 10:18 (AMPC)*

Creation is not of explicit, overt, unequivocal value in itself–especially in its current sinful, hateful, downfallen state. But it will promulgate the display of goodness and beauty before all is said and done. All the things you have come to know in abstract: goodness, truth, beauty, justice, and more – they are put on display, they are heralded, and they are best broadcast through what I've made.

Once again, I did not create out of any need within me, I did it because it accomplishes that which I esteem and value. Through it, I am putting forth that which was of the greatest goodness, truth and beauty... I am putting forth myself.

I am good and there is no good without me. Goodness is not just a characteristic of me, it is not just found within me... it does not just describe me as if it is a quality outside of me. *It Is Who I Am.* Without me, there is no goodness and nothing to tell you what is good.

Because *good* wants to distribute more goodness, I desire to distribute more of me. Before there was anything other than me... there was within me the values I wanted to transmit, focus on, and disseminate. The good of me that was within me resulted in a creation whereby those values could be shared and spread.

Let me say it more clearly...

> If there are any set of values that I want to uphold, any ideals or ethics I esteem,
>
> Any principles worth living for, any power or creativity worth displaying,
>
> Any standards worth setting apart, they are Mine!
>
> Therefore, I will live for and protect everything that I stand for. I will exercise my power and creativity. I will be jealous of everything that is good. I will be jealous for myself. I am a jealous God.

I need you to understand that when I say that I am a jealous God, it's not a bad thing. To help you understand that, I need to correct your thinking about jealousy.

There is no little green demon on my shoulder making me pout, cry, weep, and worry that you won't love me. That is not the jealousy I have: It's merely a description of how many respond emotionally to being jealous.

Jealousy is the fear of being displaced from one's RIGHTFUL position. When a woman senses her husband is growing emotionally attached to someone else, then she fears her rightful place is being threatened. In a similar way, when my people begin to give their allegiance to someone or something else, I will begin to defend my rightful place.

The problem isn't within Me, the problem is that people are often too easily satisfied with something less than the best. It's like choosing to go through the drive-thru window at McDonald's rather than a world-class buffet especially curated and prepared for them.

You see, my desire for you to have the very best and your willingness to be satisfied with something less, are at odds. Know this, I am your Creator, your provider and your sustainer. I desire to bless you and have a mutual loving relationship with you - and it is because of that, I am both angry and disappointed, when something less than the best seems satisfactory to you.

Your existence comes out of a desire, not a need, to spread my excellence and goodness in a greater way. Good desires more good. And the more that happens, the more goodness is brought into lives that can appreciate it and grow toward it. This is what makes creation a gracious decision on my part.

I love seeing my creation share in the goodness that can only be best discovered in me. It's because of this that I created a place in which my own nature is the source of your joy and goodness. What I created was out of a desire to grow goodness, not some latent *need* within me.

Despite all the goodness I created, you are keenly aware that there is now also an evil in the world.

If you are wondering how all that, which was so very good, went so very bad, then you are on the right path. Yes, the world struggles and travails...and this current battle between good and evil... it is a battle that rages on.

Creatingly yours,

—Jesus

3

The Fall and
the Beginning of Evil

Dear Jesus,

I'm still swimming around in my thoughts about the grandeur of your glory in the time before time began. And, admittedly, I'm standing in sheer wonder as I wait to see the scene you painted for when your glory will be both illuminating and penetrating throughout the new creation.

But what I still don't understand is how creation took a fall into such depravity. Given that you are a being of excellence and glory, how did we get to where we are?

If you were created to spread good, then why is there evil in the world?

Where and how do spiritual beings play a role in this?

Still standing in the wonder of you,

—Adam

Dear Adam,

I'm glad to know you are as inquisitive as ever and still have this deep-seated desire to know and seek answers.

I need to explain though – if we are going to take this journey of discovery, it needs to be done chronologically. That way you can more easily follow the events that had to transpire.

If you were going to consider constructing a grand building, you would first consult an architect to plan what was going to happen. When you read "In the beginning..." there had already been a pre-planning of that creation scene. Already the dimensions, height, and breadth of what was going to be created had been planned and considered. And already there were angels that sang of the glorious creation I was bringing into existence.

You can only dream and imagine what it must have been like to stand in the throngs of already-created beings, as I spoke your heavens and earth into existence! To have seen the emergence of the worlds, the moons, the suns, the galaxies, and the cosmos come hurling into reality out of nothingness. The glory of it all would have been something to fill every set of eyes and ears into a rapture of awe and splendor! But understand, those angels and spiritual beings observing that day were in existence BEFORE your story and your beginning.

Now, with that in mind, let me remind you–there was time between the self-existence of the Godhead... and the creation you now know.

When I created your heavens and your earth, there were witnesses to what was happening. When I began to hang suns and stars in your universe those same morning stars – or angels – began to sing (Job 38:7)!

The place of the Godhead and the glory that abounds from there is a place I created. You know it as "heaven" and it is the abode of God and the spiritual beings I created. My method of operating is that I make a place first… and then I populate it. I made heaven, and then I made angels as spiritual beings. Sometimes, I lovingly refer to them as the "morning stars." They did not have physical bodies like I designed for you. Theirs was no physical place – therefore, they had no need of physical bodies.

I created some to be messengers. Some were to be ministering spirits and others were for governing or guardianship. There were cherubim, seraphim, and others I just described as the "hosts of heaven." Yes, there were already beings in existence before those endearing words, "In the beginning."

Let me remind you about some clues I dropped along the way. When you read those first chapters of Genesis, Satan is already an existing character. He was wise as a serpent, convincing as a tempter, and he was a conniving and formidable opponent. But it took time for him to learn that because that was not the way I made him.

It took time for him to become a *fallen angel* – that was his own doing. When I created him and watched him rise in the ranks, he was truly impressive. Do you recall how I described him? I said,

> "You (Satan, Lucifer) were the signet of perfection. You were full of wisdom and perfect in beauty. You were in Eden, the garden of God and every precious stone was your covering. On the day you were created, they were prepared. You were an anointed guardian cherub. I placed you; you were on the holy mountain of God in the midst of the stones of fire, you walked.

You were perfect in all your ways from the day you
were created... UNTIL iniquity and unrighteousness
was found in you."

—*(Ezekiel 28:12-15)*

Yes, I created him, but I created him with perfection in his
beauty and placed him in a prominent position of authority and
influence. I did not create him the way he became. That was his
own doing and his own downfall. And that took time...

It took time for him to rule as the prince of the air... it took
time for the other angels to behold him and his glorious perfection...
It took time for him to consider himself and then flagrantly believe
himself to be an apt challenger to me. It took time for him to fall.

It took time for other angels and ministering spirits to form an
allegiance and an attachment to him and follow in his fall. It took
time for rebellion to grow within their ranks. Did you know that
not all the fallen angels fell at the same time, nor in the same way,
nor for the same reason? But that is a story for another time. Let's
keep our focus on the main one: Satan.

When you open the beginning pages of your Bible and are
introduced to Satan, he is already a fallen being, he is already in
rebellion. He has gone from the cherub that covers, guards, and
protects to the *tempter who tampers* with the order I set in motion
when I created.

It took time for those other angels to make similar decisions
and choices. It's amazing to me how so many can read the book I
gave them and miss these episodes within the epochs of time. But,
that too is a story for another time. Suffice it to say, there was time,
a lot of time between my creation of them, and your story that
began, "In the beginning." These beings were not created on Day
2 in your story.

Now, with all that "falling" into sin, and "falling away from me" I'm certain you will ask how and why that happened? Why did I allow it? If I'm a God who is omnipotent and omniscient, why would I permit him (and others who would follow) to be unrighteous and filled with iniquity?

So, let me explain…

What I tell you now will apply to both *you* (humanity) and *them* (the spiritual beings). So as I explain this, have it in your mind that I'm not just talking about "them" or "you." I created them without sin, but some fell. I created you without sin, and you fell too.

What I'm about to tell you is the "how" and "why" sin came into a world that I created. And take notice, Adam, each and every day's creation ended with an examination, and I declared that all I had done was *good*.

You know my character – we've already talked about this – I'm the only one that is purely and totally good. So, what happened that caused sin and rebellion to come into the worlds I made? It was not of me. I *allowed it*, but *it wasn't me*.

I had to allow it.

Let me explain.

All that happened with "evil" beginning –it didn't catch me by surprise. I knew it would happen, and I already had a plan on how to fix everything… but we need to let my plan play out as I bring all things to a culmination

Let's begin by talking about *you*. You are a person… a being with a *person*-ality. For the time being, you live in this world I created for you. In it, you live and move and have your being. But you needed a way to do all that, so I created an "earth-suit" for you. You call it your body, but you are not your body. Your body is just the "house" I prepared for you—and if I say so myself, it's quite astounding!

There will come a time when you leave the body you have, for you are in essence another spiritual being temporarily housed in that body. A spiritual being is just a personality without a physical body: they weren't made to have permanent residence in your world, they have their own realm of existence.

I made spiritual beings for the same reason I made you, to ultimately bring about *good* and to love. I have a lot of love to give, and I wanted a family to express that love to and on. They are part of my family and that's why, like you, I sometimes refer to them as "sons of God."

Now we'll get to the hard part. Ready? I don't *love* walls, rocks, planets, and suns. I love beings that can love me back. Do you remember the dog you used to love so much? Well, you didn't love a cement model of a dog—you loved a dog. You loved a dog that had personality, movement, and one who, as best he could, would love and obey you in return. Anything else is just a robot and nobody loves a robot.

And neither would I. I don't pour out my love on that which can't love me back. And yes, that means I must take the chance that some may not love me back. But what may be hard for me to express and you to understand is—*it's worth the risk.*

Knowing that only some of my creation will love me back, is worth the pain of others choosing not to love me in return. In fact, some will go far beyond not loving me to the point of actively working against me. They will refuse my care, my designs for them, my love for them, and my grand plans for them, and it will pain me deeply. But the love of those who do become part of my family *is worth the pain of those who won't.*

When I created "persons" and "person-*alities*" within the spirit world, the same rules applied. I had to give them the ability to not choose me. As much as it hurt knowing some would not, there was no other way to achieve real love for those who would. They had to not only be able to choose me, or not choose me, but they also needed to accept and take responsibility for the consequences of their choices.

Let me share an illustration that might help you understand. Imagine for a moment you are a child bouncing a ball in your home and your mom tells you not to do that because you might break a lamp. You have a choice whether you will bounce the ball or not. But, in your imagination, you think, *I'll be careful when bouncing the ball and I won't break anything.* So, you choose to continue bouncing the ball carefully, but not carefully enough. The ball hits the lamp, it teeters, and begins to fall only to find that mom has entered the room and miraculously caught the lamp before any harm was done. She scolds you and reminds you not to bounce the ball in the house and of what might happen.

However, you are surprised at how adeptly mom saved the lamp and wonder if she can do it again. So, you bounce the ball, hit the lamp, and once again it falls. And, once again, mom makes a stupendous save and the lamp doesn't break. It wouldn't take long before the whole thing would become a game to see if mom will save the lamp each and every time—and she does!

But that raises a problem, doesn't it? If mom will *always* rescue the lamp, why did she bother setting a boundary and limitation on you? Why did the ball and lamp become a moral issue of obedience if the lamp would never break? If there are no consequences for our actions, then there should never be a moral question about our actions. If there are no consequences, then you are little more than a robot that can do no harm, and that is not a loveable option.

For you to have the freedom to choose God, you must also have the freedom to NOT choose me. When I lay out moral guidelines, you must have the option of NOT following them. If you have the option of not following, then you also must be able to bear the consequences—AND THAT IS WHY THERE IS EVIL.

Yes, I am omnipotent, but I won't force you to love or obey, and you must understand there are consequences, and those consequences don't just affect you! They affect other people, often innocent people, even those people who will wonder why I allowed that to happen.

Let me get specific. My grand design was for people to know *good* and want to do good, but their choices may violate the guidelines I set in place.

I said, "Don't murder." But somebody will. They will take the life of someone else and sometimes, it's the life of an innocent someone else. Not only will their life be taken, but the pain, the loss, the stolen life taken will affect mothers, brothers, fathers, aunts, and uncles. It will affect those who might have been born in the future. It affects the possible descendants of those yet to be born, it affects friends, neighbors, work associates and more. The list just goes on and on.

Choices have consequences and ramifications: Your choices, not mine. But there's the conundrum. Many will blame me, saying if I was good, I could, and would, have stopped it. What they don't understand is *yes*, I could have stopped it. I could have prevented the circumstances and the repercussions, but here's the part they didn't think about:

If I stop all bad things from happening, then I stop *you*. I stop you from being you. I stop you from making your own decisions, your own judgments, your own choices. It means I don't allow you to do all the things you choose to do. If I stop all sin before it happens, then I stop everyone from everything and suddenly, there is no one to love for if they can't choose to sin, then they also can't choose to love me and allow me to love them.

If you understand this, then you see my predicament. I had to allow the spiritual beings to do the same thing. And some of them willingly chose their own plans, rather than mine.

Adam, in the opening pages of the "beginning" story, when you meet Satan, he is already a fallen, sinful being. He had already chosen to not only defy me, but to tempt my newest creation: "mankind." As a result, not only did he experience a fall away from me, but he took you with him.

So, yes, there was a fall among the angels, but one of the things you may need to be reminded of is that there was more than one fall in that spiritual realm. Of course, there were a number of angels that fell, but they did not all fall *at the same time, for the same reason* or *in the same way.*

Yes, there were fallen angels, but I knew it would happen, and I was prepared for it. There would come a time in the history of the world, that I would set my plan in motion, and I would fix that which was broken, repair that which had been torn down, redeem that which had fallen.

But it will take time, and that's something I have plenty of. Even if one part of my plan were to take a thousand years, it's only like a day to me (2 Peter 3:8; Psalms 90:4)

But did I set my plan in motion? Indeed, I did. I even hinted at it during my earthly life that all these things were planned from *before* the foundation of the world. Before "In the beginning" ever happened, we knew about the coming sin, we knew about the coming rebellions, and we knew we would fix, repair, renew, and re-create all things. But it would cost us something dear, and we had already planned for that too.

In my heart and that of my Father, I was already like a lamb... we considered Me already slain from *before* the foundation of the world (Revelations 13:8).

Do you understand, my incarnation, my life, my death, my resurrection – it was all pre-planned! My coming into this world, my living, my teaching, my death, burial, and resurrection was already Plan A. There was never a Plan B. Sin and its cost were necessary and painful.

Why would I do that? Why would I leave that glorious spot with all its radiant glory... and die? Because, to me, *you were worth the price.*

Let me sum things up at this point.

- Yes, I am a *good* God.
- Yes, I created all things *good.* Yes, there are spiritual beings, as well as human beings, and each is free to love and follow me, or not... and consequences for those choices will follow.
- Yes, they were already in existence before I began creating your heavens and earth.
- No, the Godhead did not need you, but we wanted you so that we could give and show our love for you... our grace to you... and our forgiveness with you and eventually exalt *good* not only in you, but throughout all creation.
- So, yes, I did (and still do) have a plan for you and a reason for your existence as well as theirs.

I did not create you because I was lonely, for I had gotten along quite well throughout all the eternity before you. I did not create you because I was somehow "insufficient"—no, it was not because I was too little, *it was because I was so much!* I had so much more to give and to share.

Adam, what you may have missed is that I wanted a family, a family I could love, a family I could share with, a family I could pour my grace upon, a family I could pour out *goodness* on, a family that would enjoy, thrive on, and distribute this goodness throughout creation.

I'm going to allow you some time to ponder what I've said, before I try to explain more. Think on these things, and when you're ready, we'll go a little further.

OK, we got through a lot of the hard stuff, but I'm sure it will lead to more questions. And I'm sure the answers you'll get will help you understand and see that indeed, there is a battle between Evil and Good, between My will, My plans, My goodness and those that choose to *neither* follow me nor love me. There is a battle that rages on…

I'm taking a risk on you,

—Jesus

4

The Other Rebellions

Dear Jesus,

My mind is spinning, maybe even bending! What did you mean there was more than one fall among the angels–that they sinned at different times, in different places and in different ways?

I haven't heard about any of that. It makes me wonder if you're joking or if it's true, *why* haven't I heard about this?

Tell me more!

—Adam

Dear Adam,

Since you raised the question, I'll be happy to share the answer, but like a flight attendant says, "Please fasten your seatbelt. The flight might be bumpy."

Of course, you already know that Satan was a very special angel. He was beautiful, artful, eloquent, powerful, and nearly perfect in all his ways, until iniquity was found in him. His beauty puffed him up and he thought more of himself than he was. He wanted to usurp my place, but I'm more than a place. I'm more than another being like him. There is none like me, but he thought it was worth a shot.

It was not.

It's interesting to watch what happens when someone takes a fall from a position of favor, and prestige. They don't want to fall alone. Especially when they imagine themselves to be in charge, an authority—a leader. Leaders are not leaders without followers, a leader isn't leading, he's just out taking a stroll.

While Satan's pride went before his fall, he did not want to go alone. There is some talk among my followers that Satan took a third of all my angels with him in his rebellion, but there's a lot of misunderstanding to the verse where they get that idea. We'll talk about that later.

For the moment, let's focus on this idea that Satan did not want to fall alone, and other angels fell away too. As I suggested previously, some of them transgressed in different ways, and at different times.

To prepare you for what I'm about to disclose, let me ask you a few questions that will help lead you to the answer. Ready?

How many female angels did I mention anywhere in your Bible? –NONE.

Are angels given in marriage? –NO.

What did the first Adam have that the angels didn't?
A WOMAN, A WIFE.

This was something new to their sight and senses. And when I told the first Adam that it was not good for him to be alone and that I would make him a woman to complete him, those angels looking on were curious, wondering and looking to see what I would create for him.

When they saw the beauty and the intrigue of the women, they wondered, *Why should only this new creation, man, have something so beautiful and we don't?* They began to covet what I created for mankind and they wanted it too. As a result, some of them decided that it was also not good for them to be alone either.

When mankind began to multiply on the face of the land and daughters were born to them, the sons of God saw that the daughters of man were attractive. And they took as their wives any they chose (Genesis 6:1-2; ESV).

And then, they preferred to stay on earth with their human wives, rather than to keep their first estate, that is, their rightful place and domain in the heavenlies.

That choice will have consequences. Remember, my decision to create included giving both angels and humans the ability to make choices different from mine, but they must also bear the consequences of those decisions.

Those angels were known as the Watchers [Daniel 4:17]. Their job was to watch over those I put under their guardianship. The offspring of those marriages were the Nephilim, or giants. Men of great stature and might. Some of the gentile nations later called them "gods" and "titans." But, while they were mighty, they were not gods to be worshiped.

These hybrid beings were an anathema, an abomination to all that I had created. These were the product of angelic beings and human beings. They were a contamination to the crowning work of what I created, and therefore I would destroy them.

This is why I told Moses and Joshua that certain tribes and peoples in the land I was giving them were to be absolutely annihilated. None of those people groups were to be left, but were to be utterly destroyed.

Adam, did you also notice that in my mercy, there were still other peoples and nations I instructed them to NOT utterly destroy? It was because the contamination of those groups had not occurred. Left unchecked, the spread of the abomination DNA would contaminate the very lineage to where and when I was going to come into the world as the Messiah.

This was a cosmic-level rebellion. Part of the problem was not only that angels made these foolish choices, but it was all part of Satan's plan to interfere with my coming as the Messiah and fulfilling the Father's plan to redeem mankind.

Go back and think it through. I was going to come into the world as a pure man: one who is all man, but also all God. For my blood to be shed for the remission of sins, it had to be pure. It was all in the plan my Father and I put together *before* the foundation of the world. I would not allow my plan of salvation for mankind to be either detoured or destroyed.

The angels that committed this atrocity had to be dealt with. I could not and would not allow them to destroy what I was pledged to do. My love for mankind would endure, and my plan for *good* to them would as well. I took appropriate steps to punish the Watchers involved as well as the off spring of the mixed beings.

I know, I know, you're wondering about whether angels had the ability to mate with human women. Let me give you a few clues:

- I never said that angels in heaven *cannot* marry, I said they *do not*.
- There are many examples I shared in your Bible of angels appearing as men.
- Some have even entertained angels and didn't know it (Hebrews 13:2).
- The men of Sodom sought to have sexual relations with two of my angels (Genesis 19:1-11), and as a result, I destroyed the entire city.

This outrage would not stand and so I removed those angels from having any future access to what I created, and I would not allow them to continue attempting to defile my plan or my people. I had them placed in bondage and in prison. They would be shuttled away to hell – far from me, my presence and my plans (2 Peter 2:4). Just as I told through Peter, I subdued them in chains in prison and in darkness. It was a place of no escape, and I will use my saints to bring judgment on them at the end of time (1 Corinthians 6:3).

I also brought Jude into my confidence and told him of the angels who did not stay within their own position of authority or kept their first estate. Instead, they left their proper dwelling, and so I kept them in eternal chains under gloomy darkness until the judgment of the great day (Jude 1:6).

And the Nephilim, the hybrid beings, I put out contracts on them. This invading unholy group was to be extinguished. It was only the groups or people who encouraged, honored and sustained them that were to be utterly destroyed.

I remember those days clearly: I saw that the wickedness of man was great in the earth, and that every intention of the thoughts of his heart was only evil continually. And I regretted that I made man on the earth, and it grieved my heart.

So I said, "I will blot out man whom I have created from the face of the land, man and animals and creeping things and birds of the heavens, for I am sorry that I have made them." But Noah found favor in my eyes (Genesis 6:5-8).

There are those who speak foolishly of my actions, as if I sinned by destroying the abomination.

They think it "ungodly" that I would bring destruction upon these groups: They like to accuse me of acting horrifically against that which was an abrogation of my *good* creation. They simply do not understand the threat of, nor the degree of, desecration being brought to my *good* creation.

Let me remind you, I exalt all that is *good*. *Good* is not just something I do, it is who I am. Goodness has its source and foundation in me. Without me, there is no *good*.

Those naysayers wave their fingers at me and try to shame me for protecting my creation. They have no concept of the dangers and threats or of the cataclysmic destruction the Nephilim and their contagion brought into the world. And it wasn't just the presence of the Nephilim: It was that entire people groups or nations had willingly invited and celebrated their presence among them. This was all part of the evil that filled the hearts of mankind and demanded that corruption should be drowned out—this was the foundation and cause of Noah's flood. This was the evil that filled mankind's hearts and minds.

The naysayers have no concept of the degree of corruption the Nephilim and the people groups descended to because they have no concept of my degree of holiness, righteousness and majesty.

The Nephilim and the sin of the Watchers was an abomination that needed to be stamped out, completely and utterly so. The sin of the Watchers had nothing at all to do with the sin of Satan, and nor did it have anything to do with the fallen angels to whom I had given guardianship of the gentile nations. I'll come back to this topic in a moment, but first more needs to be said of the sin of Satan.

Pride was not the only fault found in Lucifer (a.k.a. Satan), and the other angels who also fell. Jealousy was mixed in with it and it made a toxic combination. When I made the angelic and spiritual realm, I called the angels "sons," just like I do those of you humans that I have redeemed. They liked that, but they felt threatened to know that humanity, a creature made well after them and a little lower than them, were also going to be raised to sonship.

Mankind was created as a lower order than the angels (Hebrews 2:7), and the possibility of jealousy, outrage and pride was another poisonous recipe for the angels who may have interpreted my raising up mankind as a threat to their own positions. After all, the angels were created before mankind, and they had been given places of authority before mankind. Yet, humanity was given a position of being an image-bearer of me, ruling over the Earth and I would come to call those I redeemed "sons of God" just as I had done with them. In response, some angels rebelled in a fit of jealousy and outrage and abandoned their positions of trust and authority.

You see, in those days, I used many of them in my Divine Council. They were to assist in regulating, guarding and protecting what I created. One day, many of the saints will replace them in my Divine Council. "You will judge the earth. You will judge the angels" (1 Corinthians 6:3).

Yes, I had placed angels in places of governing, protecting, and guarding. In fact, after all the nations rejected me at the Tower of Babel, I turned those nations over to those governing angels. If you don't remember that, it's understandable. It happened a very long time ago and it is a portion of Scripture that is often overlooked, ignored or misunderstood. Even some of those who were translating my Word from one language to another missed the importance of this one.

Let me point you to a time that was after the Great Flood. Noah and his family had come out of the ark and they began to multiply, just as I had instructed. But as they multiplied, so did the hardness of their hearts and the sin that was within them. I told them to spread out on the face of the earth, but instead, they rebelled, chose their own plans rather than mine and stayed in one location.

I had to keep my work on track, and that meant these people needed to spread throughout the earth. Oh, how I remember that day. Everyone was busy with building a grand public work–they were going to build a tower to reach the heavens. Now, don't get me wrong: They knew they couldn't build a project that reached that high, but what was meant was that from the top of that tower they would *reach into* the heavens. That is, it was going to be a place of worship, but it wasn't a worship of me.

So, I did what needed to be done, and you should have seen the quizzical looks on so many faces. For, you see, I simply changed the languages of the people working there. Up until that time, there was just one people group and one language (Genesis 11). I did it without any warning and no public service announcements.

It was a little comical to watch as a man on the 17th floor of the tower who was used to laying bricks and calling out to those below to send up more, when they responded with quizzical looks as if they didn't understand him. And when they attempted to communicate as they did every other day – it was only met with more confusion. And that same chaos was being experienced on every level of the construction process.

A summary of the event could have been described by an on-looker like this: Somebody in the group got smart and yelled out, "If you can understand me, let's all go over here!" Someone else saw that and thought it was a good idea, so he did the same. In his new language he called to the crowd saying, "If you can understand me, we're all going to go to the southwest corner of the tower and we'll get away from all this chaos and insanity!" As a result, the nations, or language-groups, began to spread out on the face of the earth (Genesis 11:1-9).

So, there were about 70 groups and 70 languages that started that day... 70 that spread out where I wanted them to go all along (Genesis 10). But they were 70 rebellious, hard-hearted, disobedient groups that wanted to worship someone besides me... so, I just let them. They walked away from me with their hearts, and I walked away from them.

No, I didn't abandon them completely. After all, I still cared for my creation, but I wasn't going to waste my time on them. You need to understand, I am patient (1 Corinthians 13:4; 2 Peter 3:9; Psalms 78:41, 95:9, 106:14; Micah 2:7), but even God has an end to His patience. I put each of those groups under the tutelage of various angels (Watchers) who were supposed to guide, guard and watch over them. As usual, I dropped hints about this, but many readers miss it.

Of course, Moses mentioned it when he said that my work was perfect and all my ways were just. I am without iniquity, I am just and upright. After having said that, he reminded the people of the time I gave the nations their inheritance. That is, I gave them what they had coming... I divided mankind up into the 70 people groups and gave each of them an allotted territory. Then, I fixed those borders according to the number of the angels I set over them (Deuteronomy 32:8).

This is where some people get confused. Some of the early translators didn't understand how I could set the various nations under the oversight of my sons, or angels. So, someone edited my words to say I divided the nations according to the number of the sons of Israel. Well, that didn't make any sense at all. How did he think I was going to do that? Israel didn't exist yet. What possible relationship did those nations have with the number of the Sons of Israel who had not even yet been established as a nation yet. This occurred long before I had even approached Abram and promised him that a nation would come from him.

Adam, notice in those versions there is usually a footnote saying how the earliest manuscripts read "sons of God" or the "number of my heavenly court."

You see how easy and yet complex all the translation work is? It's something I must deal with all the time! And it's something that really tries the patience of the Holy Spirit who is the one responsible for guiding you into all Truth (John 16:13).

Anyway, back to the story. I established each of the nations (soon-to-be-called Gentile nations) under the authority of various angels. And this is where more trouble started.

Given that angels were to be responsible for watching over the people, the people naturally looked to them as authority figures. But, as people are so prone to do, they began to elevate their guardians to gods. And, those angels not only allowed it, but enjoyed it and encouraged it. As a result, they became the gods of those nations. I gave the nations up to (compared to Romans 1:26) what they wanted and I turned them over to their desire to have gods. I have a lot more to say about this... and how I handled it, but we'll have to save that conversation for another time. In the meantime, look at the times my angels appeared before men and the angels had to caution them not to worship them (Colossians 2:18; Revelations 19:10, 22:8,9; Matthew 4:9-10; Romans 1:25).

From what I've shared with you in these letters, you know that I am a Jealous God and I will not share my glory with another. These so-called "gods" would be judged. I've already called them out and given my judgment on them. No, I didn't treat them the same as those who cohabited with earthly women, but I did bring serious judgment [Jude 1:6].

I called for a special meeting in Heaven; another Divine Council meeting. I gave an entire Psalm to recall this event. The hosts of heaven were in attendance, and I told them just what I was thinking. I asked these Watchers pointedly, "How long will you judge unjustly and show partiality to the wicked?" (Psalms 82:1-2)

Then I told them where they had failed me, and my expectations of them. I told them they should have given justice to the weak and the fatherless; maintained the right of the afflicted and the destitute.

They should have rescued the weak.

I reminded them that the nations had neither knowledge or understanding, that they walked about in darkness (Psalms 82:3-5).

And then I reminded them of their positions before pronouncing their punishment. My words to them were, "You are gods, sons of the Most High, all of you; nevertheless, like men you shall die and fall" (Psalms 82:6-7).

Did you catch what I did? I took from them one of the most unique, inherent qualities about them... their immortality. They would die and fall, like men, like all earthly inhabitants. They would be gods no more (Psalms 82:6).

As for me, well, I started over. I decided that if those nations didn't want me, then I wouldn't force myself upon them. I would start fresh and make a new nation for myself. I didn't take away any of the nations from those I put in charge over them. No, I started fresh. I started with just one good man. His name was Abram and, as you know, I renamed him, Abraham. Oh, I enjoyed my time with him. I could sit and talk with him one-on-one, man-to-man so to speak. We were actually *friends* (James 2:23).

So, I chose this one man, made a covenant with him and his descendants. I *chose* Abram and I told him that his family would be special to me. I told him that they would be a people holy to me... and that I had chosen them out of all the peoples on the face of the earth to be my people and they would be a treasure to me (Deuteronomy 7:6).

Now my dealings with him are also a whole other story we might talk about at another time. For now, I must get back to answering your questions and reviewing where we are in this story.

Do you understand and see that there wasn't just one fall?

Yes, Lucifer's fall was traumatic to all of creation, but it was just the first of the falls. There was another fall I mentioned, that of the angels who kept not their first estate and abandoned their responsibilities. And there was also the fall of the angels who overstepped their authority, lorded over the nations and became objects and persons of worship. Like Lucifer, who wanted to usurp my throne, there were those who also wanted their own thrones among the nations. They accepted and sought worship and sacrifices.

They were involved in the assaults on my kingdom, my throne, my domain and my people. They became the gods of the Egyptians. They were the gods of the Babylonians, the Greeks, the Romans, the Assyrians, the Hittites, and every other nation that vaunts themselves against Me.

I hope it makes even more sense to you now when you hear how I demanded that my people not have any other gods before me and why I warned them against taking up the worship of the gods of the other nations. From the very beginning, I've wanted only *good* and the *best* for the people of my creation. That was the very purpose of my creation: to promulgate and point to that which is good and beneficial and to demonstrate that I AM the source of that goodness.

Spiritual warfare wasn't a one-time event. Indeed, no. The battle within the spiritual world as well as the battles within the physical human world are all part of the same chaos and futility that has enveloped both worlds for a very, very long time.

There were three falls that I've described and elaborated.

- The first was certainly Satan, not only falling, but also infecting humanity.
- The second involved the angels that absconded from heaven, married human women and bore Nephilim as their offspring.
- The third fall included the Watchers I set to guard and oversee the gentile nations and they accepted the worship of those nations as gods.

Don't let it depress or distress you though. Again, I knew it would happen. It was not a surprise and it did not catch me unaware, nor unprepared. I am both prepared and committed to fix the world condition... *just not yet.*

Just as there was a time to create, a time to destroy, a time for my incarnation and a time for My return... there will be a time to bring healing to the nations. There will be a time when there will be no more crying. There will be a time when tears are wiped away, that sorrow, pain, death, and hell are no more... *just not yet.*

And that's difficult for many people. They seemingly think my job is to make life safe, soft, easy and comfortable for them. And then, when trouble, crises, difficulty and tragedy hit, rather than blaming sin that was brought into the world by them, they want to blame me.

Even though you don't have all the information yet, and you don't have all your questions answered, you are nonetheless beginning to understand the why and how suffering, pain, tragedy and sin have affected the worlds I created *good.*

And in the meantime, you also need to understand that this is a "Battle That Rages On..." and it will, until the time is right—a time near the end of this age.

Waiting with you for that right time,

—Jesus

5

The Divine Council

Dear Jesus,

I noticed a phrase you used in your last communication with me. You said that you called a special meeting of a Divine Council in heaven.

That's not something I've heard about before and find it unusual to even think about. Do you mean that You, the Father and the Holy Spirit don't just decide what to do and do it?

Who would be involved in such a meeting and what kind of things are decided?

Curiouser and curiouser,

—*Adam*

Dear Adam,

I wondered if you were going to pick up on that and I'm glad you did. Explaining those meetings will help you understand other portions of your Bible, as well as understand how I work with my creation. Some of the Bible stories you are familiar with involve these meetings, but few people really catch what's going on.

OK, let's go back and think about the persons and *person*-alities in my creation. You are one and so it should be easy for you to clearly understand that you are different from all other personalities. Your experiences, your culture, your outlook, your education, your training and more have all worked together to shape the person you are. Each and every one of the beings in my creation are uniquely different and come into every situation with opinions, attitudes and outlooks that vary.

I did that on purpose. That's what's so special about each and every one of you. As you well know, I didn't make you little robots that repeat what they have been told. I like that about you, and it was what I had in mind when I created you.

This doesn't apply to just you humans: That's the way I designed the spiritual realm too. Each of the angels has their own personalities shining through everything they do. Yes, they have varying opinions on topics and ideas – and it shows.

I didn't make either you or them to just take orders. Oh, no. I designed you to think, to ponder, to discover, to create, to use the mind and instincts I gave you. And as for those who have wisdom, and use it well, I really appreciate them and I enjoy their input. I like it when someone demonstrates the ingenuity I gave them.

Let me give you a "for instance." Do you remember the story of my creation of your original namesake, Adam? I created him to take mastery over the earth and the creature inhabitants I put there. Now, think about the details of that story, think back to the time I brought to him the variety of creatures I designed, created and breathed life into.

After I designed, created and breathed life into them, what did I do? I brought them to Adam *to see what he would name them!* I didn't name them, and I didn't tell him what name to give them. I allowed him to use his own imagination, creativity and ingenuity to label them and call them as he saw fit. Out of the ground, I formed every beast of the field, and every bird of the heavens, and brought them to the man to see what *he* would call them. And whatever the man called every living creature, that was its name. The man gave names to all livestock and to the birds of the heavens and to every beast of the field (Genesis 2:19-20).

What so many people miss is that I *wanted* Adam to make some of the decisions. I gave him brain cells in his head, not transistors. I designed him to make decisions, propose ideas, form thoughts and to use these ingredients. I did the same with the angels, and that's why each of you will be responsible for your own actions and the consequences of your decisions.

Now, let's expand that thought. Just as I authorized mankind to make decisions and to act with authority in taking dominion over the earth. I *did the same thing* in the spiritual realm. Just as I use mankind to govern the earth, I use angels to govern elsewhere.

I don't *need* the input of you or them, but I take joy in watching, listening and observing my creation's thinking and actions. I not only created mankind and angels *on* purpose, I created them *with* purpose.

I've been known to call special meetings of leading angelic authorities and I've allowed their input in many decisions. Let me point out a few of those for you:

Do you remember the story of Job? He lost his possessions, his fortune, his family and his health. A lot of things happened to him. What happened to him was not by accident, and it wasn't because he deserved them. If you recall, I had called one of those special meetings in the heavens. Angels, principalities and powers were in attendance along with many of the heavenly hosts. And, yes, even Satan was among them.

There was a day when the sons of God presented themselves before Me, and Satan was among them. I said to Satan, "Where have you come from?" I don't need to get into the details of Job's story – I just wanted you to see this familiar scene, but recognize it was one of those special meetings (Job 1-2).

I like to call those meetings my *Divine Council.* It's a council meeting in heaven whereby I involve others in the governing process of what I do. Make no mistake about it: I run the show, but I enjoy the input of others.

In the next chapter of Job, you'll see a second Divine Council meeting, and once again, the angels are present and Satan walks among them again.

Maybe you can remember another one of the Divine Council meetings that took place. I needed to do something with an incredibly evil and inadequate king named Ahab. He promoted the worship of the false god, Baal. He persecuted and killed my prophets, and he refused to heed the prophetic warnings given to him. The situation had gotten so bad, I had to step in and remove him. Yes, you read that right. I was not only going to remove him from the throne he sat on, but from life itself. I made that decision, but I inquired of the council as to how they thought that might happen.

There I was, on my throne and all the hosts of heaven were standing by Me, planning, propositioning and on both, my left and my right.

I asked, "Who will entice Ahab, that he may go up and fall at Ramoth-Gilead?" That was followed by a lot of talk and discussion among those in attendance as planning, propositioning and pondering was taking place.

Then, a spirit came forward and stood before me, saying, "I will entice him" (1 Kings 22).

It was an idea he thought up on his own, so I asked how he was proposing to accomplish this. Interestingly, this spirit had come up with a good plan and I authorized him to put it into practice. And he did.

Look at what happened, Adam. Action was needed. I called a meeting and allowed spiritual beings to take part in the decision-making process. They used their thinking, their wisdom, their ideas and made suggestions.

No, this isn't so strange. I've often involved others in what I do. I enjoy having them with me, learning and growing just like you do in your own lifetime.

Let me point out another occasion when I was working and creating and I desired to involve others. Just before I created your namesake, the first Adam, I decided on what I was going to do, but I wanted my council to know and be involved. Now, make no mistake about it: I am the only Creator, but they were with me. Now pay close attention to the words I used as I began. I said, "Let us make man in our own image."

Some like to say that the "us" was a conversation amongst the Godhead, (the Father, Me and the Holy Spirit), but maybe they just haven't understood how I work.

It was also this Council that was called to order when I charged some of the angels with dereliction of duty. They had been given guardianship over the nations as you read in the previous chapter. But those angels failed miserably and acted as gods to the nations. They went so far as to receive worship and sacrifices from the people. They were intercepting and interfering with my plan to offer the people that which was "Good" and "Best". Instead, these angels were usurping my plan and implementing their own, and this was not in mankind's best interest: it wasn't "Good".

If you recall, I wrote to you previously about that, and the entire episode was written up in Psalm 82. It was time to judge those who had betrayed my trust and overstepped their boundaries as guardians. Do you remember? I didn't just call them before me and pass judgment on them. No, all of this took place at a Divine Council meeting. The Psalmist said so in his opening line (Psalms 82).

This may surprise you, but there were several Divine Council meetings that had human, earthly attendees. This was one of the marks that often distinguished my real prophets from the false ones. Yes, there were occasions when I called a Divine Council and invited earthly people to observe. I'm guessing the look on your face as you read that was incredible!

So, let me call one of those occasions to your attention. Surely, you are familiar with one of my major partners among the prophets, Isaiah. There was a lot happening on Earth at that time. I had called for a Divine Council meeting, and I invited Isaiah to attend.

It made quite the impression on him. He wrote considerably about it and tried as best he could to describe it. Words failed him somewhat, but he still did a good job. He was amazed at what he had seen as he peered at Me. He just couldn't get over the majesty, the pomp and circumstance.

In his attempt to describe what he experienced he said that he saw me once again, sitting on my throne. My position was high and lifted up and the train of my robe filled the temple. Above me were the seraphim. Each had six wings: with two they covered their faces; with two they covered their feet and with two they would fly. The anthem was playing, the angels were singing and the words describing me were "Holy, Holy, Holy" [Isaiah 6].

Did you think this was a dream he was having? No! No! – He never said he was asleep… He just said that he saw Me. It was a Divine Council and I called him to be an observer and participant. A participant? – Yes. I asked the question, "Who will go for us?" and I saw him boldly raise his hand as he volunteered, "Here am I, send me!"

As I mentioned, I did this with several of my prophets throughout history, even the Apostle Paul. It was an event he never forgot. Fourteen years after it happened, he was still talking about it. He spoke about how he had been caught up into heaven. It really shook him up… he didn't know if he was in his body or out of it. He heard things there that he was never able to communicate to others (2 Corinthians 12:2-4).

Now, I want to remind you that this is not something so rare that it will never be done again. No, Adam, open your mind and recall I said that many of you who follow me, who live for me and who may die for me will be called upon, and honored, with being able to rule and reign with me.

Don't you understand, I want so much more for you than just "getting you into heaven." I have plans for you, hopes for you. I want you to grow, learn, offer your ideas and your thinking throughout time to come. You are NOT going to go to heaven, sit on a cloud, play a harp and sing all day long! Even I must admit that it just sounds pathetically boring!

No, I want you to think. I want your planning. I want you to have more than knowledge. I want you to grow in wisdom so you can offer input, ideas, challenges, plans and more! Grow up, Adam... and keep on growing! Develop your heart for me and then add your mind as well. I gave you that mind so you could – and would – use it. Use it for my glory! Come on Adam, I have big plans, and I want you involved!

Inviting you,

—Jesus

PS: You need to know that this kind of thinking and plan-ning is also an ingredient in those who have rebelled against and betrayed me. Satan, and others, have been making their own plans, throwing out their own ideas and they also want to be involved in decision-making. But their involvement is treacherous, deadly and conniving. They still work to destroy me, My kingdom and the good' I have laid up for you. Their insurgence, agitation, betrayal, duplicity, infidelity, and uprising is not over.

Their insurrection and their evil intent means "The Battle Rages On..."

6

The Jealousy of God

Dear Jesus,

You recently mentioned that you are a jealous God and I remember reading that a few times in the Bible. I thought being jealous was not a good attribute, and it was something we *don't* want to be. Being jealous seems self-centered and egotistic. How can a holy and loving God be jealous?

—Adam

Dear Adam,

As usual, you ask good questions, and as you know, I try to give good answers to good questions. Before I get started, let me remind you that my goal has always been to spread and enlarge all that is *good.*

Goodness has its roots in me. *Good* wants to multiply itself and spread that *goodness.* This is what I do, and it's the very heart and reason I created in the first place.

Let's take just some of my attributes and put them in a box... and see what we have:

God's Attributes, or The Jesus Box

Faithful, Forgiving, Glorious, Good, Grace, Gracious, Helpful, Honest Honor, Honorable, Immutable, Incorruptible, Integrity Irreproachable, Just, Justice, Kind, Love, Loveable, Lovely, Loving, Mercy, Merit, Moral Excellence, Nobility, Noble, Omnipotent, Omnipresent, Omnipresent, Patient, Perfection, Pleasant, Praise, Praiseworthy, Principled, Probity, Propriety, Pure, Pureness, Purity, Rectitude, Respectable, Right, Righteous, Safe, Savior, Self-Sufficient, Sovereign, Transcendent, True, Trust, Trusting, Trustworthy, Truthfulness, Uprightness, Venerable, Virtue, Wholesome, Wise, Worthy

Adam, look at what's in the box. This is me. This is what I uphold. This is who I am. I am the source of all these things that are admired and sought after. When someone rejects me, they may not realize it, but they are rejecting the source of all these glorious attributes. They don't understand that what they want are these qualities, but without me, it is impossible.

For these things to be available to them, they must choose me. And here's the thing: *I want them to have these.* I want them to be available. I want them to want me. Why? So they can have these attributes in their own lives! In being a jealous God, I am jealous to share these with you! When I do, I'm sharing myself with you, and that's why I am a jealous God. Providing myself is the best thing I can do for humanity.

Previously, I wrote to you about some of the guardian angels abusing their authority, abandoning their responsibilities and over-stepping the bounds of what they had been assigned to do. They had become the gods of the gentile nations.

I think I need to explain a few things at this point. First, how do I define a god? I've heard a few of your friends chatting about football or money being a god. No, these are not gods. People don't worship football or money. Yes, they may spend a lot of time and money enjoying football and they may invest an inordinate amount of effort in accumulating riches, but those are not gods.

A god is a being, a personality: one that ranks above you on the created level. They may have more knowledge, more abilities and more authority than humanity. Recognizing this, people have tried to influence them by appealing to them through devotion, gifts, sacrifices and even loyalty. Their goal is to use the power, influence or knowledge of their god to abate evil and acquire good. Do you understand that they seek *good*, but they try to find it outside of me.

There is often a symbiotic relationship between the god and the person. People appeal to, and give gifts to, the god(s) in an effort to persuade them to provide good for the people.

There is a ranking of order within creation. You (humanity) were made a little lower than the angels. When I took on flesh, I came into humanity as one of you. In doing so, I was for a little while lower than those angels (Hebrews 2:7-9). That's not to say you remain there, not at all, for I have called you to be "saints" and "sons" and sometimes I even referred to you as my "bride." And we've already covered how you will be called upon to judge both, the earth and angels.

I commissioned some of those angels to watch over the gentile nations. Again, the gentile nations are those that are not Israel, those I have not made a covenant with and are not my beloved Israel. No, Israel is mine. I did not put her under the authority of anyone else. I chose her to do something special that will bless all the other nations. It's all part of my plan.

When the nations abandoned me, I turned my attention to making my own nation and making my own covenant with Israel (Deuteronomy 32:9).

As I've already taught you, those guardian and watchful angels then trespassed into the area of becoming gods to the nations they were only to watch, serve and guide.

Instead, the nations that refused Me so long ago, continue to refuse Me now. They seek *goodness* through the gods rather than me.

When angels place themselves in positions whereby people seeking good would call upon them instead of me, that is an abomination.

That is an abortion of what the entire process of Creation was to give birth to: seeking me and spreading my goodness throughout all that I made. Seeking *good* was to bring people to me, not them. When they interfered in this and substituted themselves for me, it was an anathema.

Why is it an anathema? It's not because I'm on an ego trip. It's not because I need your attention and adoration. It's because I am the source of what you are seeking, and you can't find it anywhere else, not even in them! Please understand that my jealousy is for your own good. It's for your Good, that I keep the source of good available to you, and not a cheap, short-sighted imitation of my goodness.

People are so dear to me. They are the crown of my creation in this realm. I love them so much, I even dared to take on flesh and die for them. I want them in my life. I desire them. I seek them. I search for them. I want the good and the best for them, and I will fight for them!

I am being jealous for my own glory. I will not allow another to usurp it!

At this point, you need to acquire a better understanding of what it means for me to be jealous. I not only said that I was a jealous God, but I used that term as one of my names, so you'd better understand this is a part of my nature and my being (Exodus 34:14).

I told Moses (and had him to write it down) that I was a jealous God. It was carved into stone so you couldn't miss the message. When I gave him the commandments, I included with the prohibition of worshiping other gods that statement that I was a jealous God.

I told the people, "You shall not make for yourself a carved image, or any likeness of anything that is in heaven above, or that is in the earth beneath, or that is in the water under the earth. You shall not bow down to them or serve them, for I, the LORD, your God, am a jealous God" (Exodus 20:4-5).

Yes, I realize that you usually associate being jealous with bad traits. It's not something you want to be guilty of. But, when you rightly understand it, jealousy is a good trait. So, let me explain.

When someone is jealous, it is most often associated with threatening their ego. With me, it's a threat to my rightful position. If I wasn't rightfully jealous of my position with you, then I would allow you to reach for something that isn't in your best interest.

You need to understand, I'm jealous for my own glory because I want to give you what is best for you. I want to give you Me. I don't want you settling for something less than the best and if you reach for and worship something else: it cannot compare with me. For me to give you what is best, *I must give you myself* and I will not allow anyone or anything else to diminish that. It's for your sake I do this.

Don't you know that all creation functions best when my glory is the focal point of their existence? Man is never happier, he's never more satisfied, he's never more fulfilled, life is never more pleasant than when I am the center of their existence, and they are enjoying me!

- You'll be the happiest you can be when your focus is on me.
- You'll be the best person you can be when your focus is on me.
- Your marriage will be the best, your parenting will be the best, your singleness will be the best it can be when your focus is on me. I have *you* in mind when I say I am a jealous God.

Maybe you're starting to get the picture? If so, you'll know then that my jealousy is so strong that when another being attempts to usurp my position and receive worship from you, then my longing and desire for *your best* kicks in and I take corrective measures.

This was a big deal and there were some cataclysmic effects. With that in mind, I'm surprised that not many people give attention to it. But once again, I had it written down in my book so you and others could read it for yourselves.

I called a Divine Council and I called these wannabe "gods" onto the carpet to give an account and to receive judgement for their actions.

Of course, I want my people to love me in return, but for there to be love, one must have the ability to choose my will or their own. And, whichever they choose, there will be consequences. And there were to be consequences for those who wanted to be your "gods."

Before I go into what happened, let me remind you that I loved those angels. As you may have read, before the foundations of the world, I determined the number of the stars (another favorite term I had for my angels) and I gave and called them all by name (Psalms 147:4).

I created them in varied splendor, rank and authority... and some were chosen to assist in ruling and reigning my creation. Some would be angels and fewer would be authorized as archangels. They were given responsibilities and authority commensurate with their abilities. Some would carry out missions and others would assist me in the giving of missions and work through the Divine Council that we've already spoken about.

My Father and I are absolute, sovereign and reign over all – but we are also love. We love all that we made, and each of them was only endowed with *good*... I pronounced them as good.

But they were also endowed with another trait, a very dangerous trait... "freedom." I gave them the freedom to make choices. They were not God-controlled, they weren't mechanical. You know I couldn't love something, or someone, like that. They would lack personality, choice, decision-making and the ability to choose Me. No, I gave them abilities, discernment, room for knowing and growing... and room for denying.

As they matured, I would appoint some to positions of authority... some to share in my ruling and reigning... just like I've promised to do for you, and others who follow Me. I did tell you that you would be ruling and reigning with me... do you remember? I specifically told Paul to pass this on to Timothy and I'm sure it was shared with you. I said that if you endure hardship for me, you will rule with Me (2 Timothy 2:12).

If you're keeping up with me, you know I loved those angels... and I had great plans for them, but they made choices, and those choices had consequences. Let me take you back there... to the time I called a Divine Council and I called them onto the carpet. I asked them plainly,

> "How long will you judge unjustly and show partiality
> to the wicked? You should have been giving justice
> to the weak and the fatherless; you were supposed to
> maintain the right of the afflicted and the destitute.
> You were supposed to rescue the weak and the needy;
> and deliver them from the hand of the wicked."
>
> *(Psalms 82:2-4).*

And having said all that, I ended with passing a judgment on them that I'd never had to use before. I created them as non-corporeal beings, spirit-beings, beings without a physical body and without birth. They were to be immortal. Being spirit and without a body that would decay, they were to live forever. But, their lack of reverence for me and my position, their abandonment of why I put them in the positions they had, their failure to take care of my precious people... well, it brought me to a point where I had to bring just judgment. With that, I had to say,

"You are gods, sons of the Most High, all of you; nevertheless, like men you shall die, and fall like any prince."

—*Psalms 82:6-7*

It was a sad day in heaven. But there was rejoicing that justice was done.

A direct attempt to undermine my glory or to thwart my position and my plans will not be tolerated. My purpose in creation was to expand Good. The plan for people was to show them that which is Good and allow them to choose it and then find it in me. That is the overarching purpose of all that I've done.

The interference that has occurred... the rebellions that took place... the insidious schemes that sought to eliminate what I predetermined and predestined will not be tolerated, but they don't surprise me either.

My Father and I preplanned the path we desired for creation *before* I spoke a single word of creation into existence. We already knew that rebellion and sin would be a problem, but we also knew what we would do about it.

We knew, we planned, we strategized... we predestined that I would take on flesh... I would become one of you. I would show you what *good* looks like. I would offer good to you by offering you myself. And in demonstrating that *goodness*, I would die for you.

People being redeemed, saved and being born-again was never "Plan B." It wasn't as if I made an inadequate world and sin destroyed my plan. No! We knew sin would happen. We knew angels would fall. We understood the consequences and we felt the agony of being rejected... but it didn't surprise us. It didn't sneak up on us. And those who find me are worth the risk and the pain of the rejection by some.

No, my coming in the flesh was "Plan A" all along. Offering myself and my *goodness* was always the goal. And it was never our plan to repair a broken earth; it was always to redeem it and recreate it!

The world started with Me. I created it. And it will end with Me. I will re-create it. This is why I'm known as the *Alpha and Omega,* the *first and the last,* the *beginning and the end!* I am on both ends of creation!

The universe is mine... both the spiritual and the physical. I created it. There was nothing that was created except that it was created by me (John 1:3-5).

THIS IS WHY I AM A JEALOUS GOD!

And because everything that is Good is within me, I want to share it all with all my creation. Not just you... not just the angels. No, no – that is far too short-sighted.

When *all* things are completed, *all creation* will rejoice. It's been foretold... and it's all in the book.

The day is coming when I will hear *every creature in heaven and on earth and under the earth and in the sea,* and all that is in them, saying, "To him (that's me) who sits on the throne and to the Lamb be blessing and honor and glory and might forever and ever!" (Revelations 5:13)

When you think about this, it should make more sense when you read what I told the apostle Paul about how all things are waiting in great anticipation for this event:

"For you know that the whole creation has been groaning together in the pains of childbirth until now. And not only the creation, but you, yourselves, who have the first-fruits of the Spirit, groan inwardly as you wait eagerly for adoption as sons, the redemption of your bodies."

—Romans 8:22-23

Look again at what I said, the whole of creation is eagerly awaiting the day. The beasts of burden, the fish within the sea, the wild creatures and even those that fly… they are all awaiting the day I finish what I started "In the beginning…"

What are they waiting for? – They're waiting for the contents of My box to permeate everything and everyone.

Remember the box? It's Me! It's what I'm jealous for! And it's for your sake that I am!

The Jesus Box

Faithful, Forgiving, Glorious, Good, Grace, Gracious, Helpful, Honest, Honor, Honorable, Immutable, Incorruptible, Integrity, Irreproachable, Just, Justice, Kind, Love, Loveable, Lovely, Loving, Mercy, Merit, Moral Excellence, nobility, Noble, Omnipotent, Omnipresent, Patient, Perfection, Pleasant, Praise, Praiseworthy, Principled, Probity, Propriety, Pure, Pureness, Purity, Rectitude, Respectable, Right, Righteous, Safe, Savior, Self-Sufficient, Sovereign, Transcendent, True, Trust, Trusting, Trustworthy, Truthfulness, Uprightness, Venerable, Virtue, Wholesome, Wise, Worthy

But, once again, I need to warn you… not all of creation is choosing me or the *good* that is within Me.

Those that are against me are nefarious… they plot and plan in the dark. They too offer a box. and while their box is decorated oh-so-nicely, it's what's inside that is poisonous. The decorations look appealing – just as the fruit did to Eve. Adorned with what looks good, it's what's inside that is malignant and deadly.

The Box of Every Other God

Steal, Kill, Destroy, Adultery, Atrocious, Corrupt, Coveting, Crime, Deceit, Demonic, Diabolical, Dreadful, Egregious, Evil, False Witness, Faults, Fiend, Foul, Godless, Heinous, Immoral, Impiety, Impropriety, Impure, Iniquity, Liar, Malevolent, Malicious, monstrous, Murder, Nefarious, Obscene, Odious, Offense, Outrage, Reprehensible, Satan, Sin, Tempter, Transgression, Trespass, Ugly, Ungodly, Vice, Vile, Villain, Wicked, Wrong, Obscenity, Odiousness, Satanic, Sinful, Sinister, Temptation, Ugliness, Usurper, Violent, Wickedly, Wrongful, Vicious… and so much more.

The gods are masters at tempting, alluring and deceiving… but the outside can't hide the stench of what's inside…

There are those who have a different agenda, a different plan, and different gods. And they are not at rest. They are planning and plotting against all that I am and all that I plan. They don't want you to have my Box… they don't want you to find yourself in me. It's been that way from nearly the beginning, and it will continue until all creation is recreated by me, not even heaven is immune to "The Battle That Rages On…."

Passionately jealous for my own glory, for your sake,

—Jesus

7

What is Spiritual Warfare?

Dear Jesus,

Let me recap what I think you've said. I want to be sure I am understanding it all… but I still have questions too.

What you've taught me so far includes that you are not only "Good", but that "Goodness" has you as its source. Without you, no one would know what *good* is. I've also learned that you created the worlds that exist as your means of spreading your "Goodness" because "Good" loves to multiply "Goodness".

I've also picked up the idea that Satan fell from grace and fellowship with you, but he wasn't alone. Other angels also made choices that made them enemies to you. They left their rightful places and responsibilities; they took up residence on Earth and they took wives from the human race.

The union of spiritual beings (who can take on the appearance of mankind) and human beings resulted in genetic chaos that was an abomination to you. To protect what you created, you then brought judgment upon the angels that left their first estate and put them in chains in darkness where they await further judgment.

You've shown me that there was a third failing among the angels. The angels you assigned as Watchers to oversee the affairs of the gentile nations trespassed by elevating themselves from merely being Watchers to serving as gods to those nations.

I understand that you gave both, angels and humans, the opportunity to make decisions. Those decisions will bear consequences and set destinies. You did it because you wanted beings to love and to choose to love the good they can find in you. It was a risk to do this because they could choose not to follow or love you – and many did. But, the love you receive and give to those who *do* choose you is worth the risk – and the pain – of those who do not.

But what I'm not clear about is why there is spiritual warfare and *how* spiritual warfare takes place. I mean, is there a point to all this rebellion?

I really need some help seeing how all this works.

—Adam

Dear Adam,

You certainly have great focus. You're asking some very good questions, and I want to help you understand. In doing so, let me begin by telling you what spiritual warfare is *NOT*. Once you know what it is not – you'll be better equipped to discover what it *IS*.

"Spiritual warfare" is understood by some to refer to the encountering of demonic and angelic spirits... and to others, it's little more than facing life's struggles, whether they be political, economic, or just putting up with unfriendly people and bad traffic.

Some believers go so far as to link bad weather, bad news, a bad economy and even bad breath with spiritual warfare. But sometimes, bad breath is just a lack of good oral hygiene, not the presence of an unholy spirit.

Sometimes, financial distress is just a foolish decision in handling money... not "the devil." Sometimes, bad traffic is just a distracted driver on the highway... not a highway demon. Sometimes, life's struggles with others are the result of not using wise and gentle words. Sometimes, an enemy is formed by harsh words and attitudes... not because of spiritual warfare. And sometimes, people just say and do stupid and foolish things... or they follow their own desires instead of mine and blame the consequences of their actions, their words and their lack of wisdom on the demonic world.

Too much is being shoved into the tent called "spiritual warfare" and yet, few really understand the reality and the authority of the principalities, powers, rulers of darkness and spiritual wickedness in high places. or their limitations.

As I explained in a previous letter, spiritual beings are persons with personalities. They have experiences, make decisions and they live and work mostly in a world unlike yours. Having the ability to make choices results in having the responsibility to accept the consequences of those choices.

Their enmity against me has carried on almost since the beginning of time. As we've discussed in our correspondence, Satan was the first to fall from grace and from fellowship with me.

It wasn't long before he was also trying to interfere and destroy for mankind. He chose his words carefully and enticed Eve and Adam to doubt my word and disobey my directions. He was crafty and he has been carrying on that same work throughout the ages.

He has prepared many plans to derail, delay and destroy all that I intended. For instance:

- It was within his plans to raise up the Nephilim – the children of the angels who married earthly women. They were a plague to the Israelites. It was an attempt to destroy the people I chose to represent me on planet Earth.

- It was the prince of darkness's strategy to kill the Israelite babies in Egypt and prevent my people from becoming a successful nation. You do remember that Egypt had many false gods, don't you? – When the Israelites' population began to grow, who do you think influenced them to enslave the nation and kill the babies?

You know Lucifer as the "Prince of the Power of the air" and other powerful former angels as principalities and powers.

- It was them that persuaded nations to fight against Israel, to carry away their wise and strong sons… to harass and to pillage the various tribes of my nation.

- It was under their persuasion that the god, Dagon, tried to humiliate me by bringing my Ark of the Covenant into his temple, but you saw that while I might allow my people to be tested, I would not allow a god like him to hold me in disdain. Do you remember that I made him tumble, and broke him into pieces (1 Samuel 5)?

- It was they that inspired the killing of my prophets, the scattering of Israel and the exile of Judah.

- It was their influence that sought to delay my messengers to the prophet Daniel, and it was their plan to kill Shadrach, Meshach and Abednego (Daniel 3).

- It was a strategy dreamed up in hell to persuade King Herod to attempt the killing of me when I was still in my mother's arms (Matthew 2:16).

- It was deceit of the prince of the power of the air that led to my own people wanting to throw me off a cliff and silence me (Luke 4:29).

- It was their treachery that deceived people to want to stone me to death before it was my time (John 8:59).

- It was the hate within Satan and the principalities that finally convinced Jewish religious leaders that they were doing a good thing when they chose to crucify me.

- And it will be this same duplicity that convinces a world to follow Satan's false prophet and anti-Christ in the last days.

Oh yes, they've been busy for a very long time. Their skill and cunning to deceive, perplex, confuse, betray, swindle, misinform, hoodwink, defraud, delude and dupe has been perfected through the ages.

Is it any wonder I had Paul to warn you that you are not wrestling with flesh and blood, but principalities, powers and spiritual wickedness in high places? Did you think the descriptive word "powers" was a misnomer? Just a poetic depiction?

Is it any wonder I warned you to guard your heart and your mind (Proverbs 4:23; 2 Thessalonians 2:2)? The mind is one of the most important battlegrounds. Many wars are won and lost in the mind before they ever get to the battlefield (Colossians 1:21; 1 Corinthians 14:14-15, 2:16).

Yes, Adam... there are battles being fought all around you that you don't see or hear. Maybe you remember the occasion when a great number of enemies were facing my prophet Elisha and his servant. I remember how amazed the servant was when I opened his eyes so that he could see the hordes of my armies mounted and protecting them from the invisible realm (2 Kings 6:17).

It was well said that "the mind is a terrible thing to waste." And it's true, but some minds are like cement, thoroughly mixed up and permanently set. Some become so hard, permanent and debased, that even God gives up on them (Romans 1:28, 7:23). And that was my motivation for encouraging everyone to love the Lord your God with all your heart and with all your soul and with all your *mind* (Matthew 22:37).

Let's keep moving and see what else they've been up to through the ages. In my previous letter, I filled you in about other angels falling too. They married and mixed with humanity and set about a process through which all mankind would be affected and infected. Their actions brought about an abhorrent calamity of beings that brought chaos and abomination into my world (Genesis 6).

When I turned the nations over to the Watchers, I also gave them authority to fulfill their responsibilities. Paul reminded you that redeemed humanity wrestles against them. My enemies have gone by many names and descriptions, including: rulers, authorities, cosmic powers, spiritual forces, principalities, powers, rulers of the darkness, spiritual hosts of wickedness in the heavenly places, world forces, authorities of the unseen world, evil spirits and demons.

My enemies are networked together into a world-wide empire. They have been for ages, and they continue to grow in their aspirations against all that is holy… all that is in my "Good" box… all that is Me and Mine. I've called their work "the spirit that is now at work in the sons of disobedience" [Ephesians 2:2].

Is it working… oh yes, it's very effective. And it leaves many people almost double-minded, but they need to know that to set the mind on the flesh is death, but to set the mind on the Spirit is life and peace. For the mind that is set on the flesh is hostile to God, for it does not submit to God's law; indeed, it cannot (Romans 8:6-7).

It's why I encouraged Paul to give warnings to my followers not to conform to this world, but be transformed by the renewal of your mind, that, by testing, you may discern what is the will of God, what is good and acceptable and perfect (Romans 12:2).

Throughout history, the power of the Godhead has put ideas, dreams and prompts into the minds of people like Peter when he shouted out in recognition of me. Do you remember he made the proclamation that I was the Christ, the son of the Living God? With that, I congratulated him and told him that he did not come to that conclusion on his own, but that my Father in heaven revealed that to him.

And there was also the time I dispatched one of my angels to put a lie into the minds of King Ahab's counselors and Ahab, himself. (1 Kings 22)

In the same way, my enemies can do the same thing. They pour lying and deceitful influences into the hearts and minds of people who do not know me. It was often done through those who said they loved God, but they were not of Him. I called them out on this occasionally, like I did when I told some of the religious rulers in Jerusalem that their father was the Devil. No, I didn't pull any punches that day (John 8:44)!

This is also what happens when a demon-spirit enters a person... and when a fortune-teller gives out their predictions.

Yes, there's a lot that happens in the spirit world that lies unseen unto even the keenest of observers. That's why on another occasion when my followers seemed powerless against them, I stepped in and had to both encourage and teach the disciples that some spirits only respond to prayer and fasting.

Under the influence of these powers, great men have been known to do great harm. They are adept at stealing the minds of humanity and deceiving them with all sorts of lies. Much destruction has occurred by those who think they are doing right, but it is the influence, lies, guile and deception by the enemy who persuades them.

Remember the boxes? – My box is filled with glory, honesty, truth, beauty and more. It's filled with everything that is good.

The box of the other gods is filled with all that is heinous, depraving and evil. It's just that they decorate their box with such appeal, it fools the fool who lingers with it until they want it no matter the cost. Again, it's very rare that evildoers choose to do evil. Instead they are fooled into doing evil by thinking it is good. And don't forget, there is no 'Good' without Me.

You used to watch a television show called, "Let's Make A Deal" where people would bring silly things in hopes of trading them for a delightful deal of money or great prizes. But there was also the prospect of winning a disappointment rather than a prize. There was one contestant who, instead of going home in a brand-new car, won a live donkey. What disillusionment! Adam, that's what my enemies offer… hopes and dreams that result only in disappointment, despair and destruction.

We are in a war setting. We have enemies who battle for your mind and your heart. They are skilled adversaries, crafty opponents and they fight, not only for your life and your future, but theirs too. They know that at the end of time they will face a final judgment, and the sentence is damning and eternal. Adam, I can't stress this enough… the battle rages on.

Ever mindful of you,

—Jesus

8

Of Giants and Mountains

Dear Jesus,

Can we go back and focus on something you mentioned that I'm having a bit of trouble understanding?

While I get that there is a realm of spiritual beings and some of them sinned by rebelling against you, there are still some things I'm still having a problem following.

It's those giants that you spoke of and how they had to be eliminated. Can you tell me more about them because that's just something I haven't heard much about, yet you seem to be making a big deal about it.

Seeking answers and clarity,

—Adam

Dear Adam,

So good to hear from you again… and so soon. That means your curiosity is working well and you are eager to learn. Good for you! Let's see if I can satisfy that appetite.

Those giants were a problem for those who lived among them then, as well as those who only read about them now.

As you've learned, the giants mentioned in the Bible were the product of rebellious and sinful angels marrying human women. Their children were the giants. I'm sad to say it, but many "scholars" have tried making the Bible story say and mean something very different from what it plainly speaks about. So, let me tell you what really happened and what it led to.

Some of this is repeating what I've said before, but please bear with me. Spiritual beings were known to take the form of human beings. That's why Paul stated that some people had entertained angels and weren't even aware of it. That's why the inhabitants of Sodom sought to "entertain" the two angels I sent there to observe and to eventually destroy the city. That's who the women saw at my tomb after my resurrection. My angels have often made personal appearances.

Now let's get to the more complicated part and see if I can walk you through it. When the angels mated with the women, the essence of the angelic beings is that they were immortal spiritual beings who took on the form of flesh. Their wives were mortal physical beings who were truly in the flesh.

This union made children who were hybrid – spirit beings mixed with human beings. This abnormal and incongruous mix had unorthodox properties. Physically, they were giants. These are the ones the 12 Israelite spies discovered in the Promised Land and most of the spies were overly fearful of them. You'll find Nephilim mentioned in several places in the Bible. You probably know some of them by name: Goliath (who is probably the most famous), Ish-bi-Benob, Saph (aka Sippai), Lahmi and the largest of them, Og who was king in Bashan.

While the people they lived among hailed them as heroes, my people, the Israelites, saw them as an ungodly enemy. Many think this is where the Greeks and others got the idea of the Titans among their gods.

There were writers, other than the Bible authors, who have told the stories of just how vile and ghastly these giants could become, but that's another story. Let's stick with what I've shared with you in the Bible.

You might find it interesting to learn that Goliath was from Gath, just one of the five cities in the Philistine pentapolis. He lost his head, literally, in that fight. But Goliath had four brothers and it was customary in that day to exact vengeance on those who kill someone close to you. That's why David picked up five stones when he was preparing to battle Goliath. He was ready in case Goliath's brothers came after him for vengeance.

Hopefully, your curiosity has been stimulated and your mind was wondering "Why would a Gathite fight for the Philistines?" And that's a good question, but it has a very simple answer: Goliath was a mercenary. A mercenary is just a professional soldier who is paid to fight. That wasn't uncommon at all, either then, or now.

Because of the size, strength, ferociousness, and aggressiveness of these giants, they gained a great deal of admiration. To a degree, they were the celebrities of their day and one of them even became a King. I mentioned his name earlier and I bring it up again now for a very good reason.

King Og was king in Bashan. This was an area in the far northeast corner of the land. King Og didn't have the publicity program Goliath did, so he isn't as famous as Goliath, but he was quite well-known and greatly feared at the time.

I sent my Israelite warriors out against Og. They went up along the road toward Bashan where Og and his army marched out to meet them for battle. Moses and others were fearful, so I reassured them when I told them not to be afraid of him, for I would deliver him into their hands, along with his whole army and his land.

Moses knew some things about Og that you may not. He was no ordinary man, but he was the last of the giants and his life would be required of him.

Og was truly gigantic by your standards. His bed was made of iron and measured 9 cubits by 4 cubits. That's about 13 feet long and 6 feet wide.

When I said Og was king in Bashan, that might not mean much to you, but it is important, and you'll understand that when I take your imagination to that place. The kingdom of Bashan included Mt Hermon and significant things happened there that you may not have put together in your own thinking yet. So, let me help you with that.

Mt Hermon is the spot where Jacob saw a ladder from which angels were ascending and descending to and from heaven (Genesis 28:10-19). It was the same place from where the Watchers made their fateful decision to mate with earthly women and it was also the location of Caesarea Philippi, which was a hot spot for the worship of the false gods. It had once been known as the Mount of God, but later was the worship center of those false gods, especially Pan, whom many theologians equate with Satan.

Why is this important? Well, when you pool all these pieces of information together, you find a strong link between some of the most un-holy beings. Mt Hermon was a hatching place for the hellish plan of the fallen angels, as well as a major center for the worship of false gods.

With that background, let me give you some more significant data: this is where I took my disciples to make an important announcement. Let me show you how all these puzzle pieces fit together.

When I took the disciples to Caesarea Philippi, I asked them, "Who do the people say I am?" They answered, saying that some thought I was John the Baptist, some Elijah and others thought I was Jeremiah or one of the other prophets (Matthew 16:13).

So, I got more to the point and asked them who *they* thought I was. That's when Peter made his great declaration and said I was the Christ, the Messiah, the Son of God! That was very insightful for him, and I certainly congratulated him, letting him know that God was working in him and revealed that to him (Matthew 16:13-17).

I'm certain you remember that story... but I'm guessing you didn't equate it with the location being that same Mt Hermon, where the rebellious angels made their plans... or with Bashan, the place of King Og... nor of Pan, and his association with Satan. You might say this was the earthly Headquarters of the unholy.

And it was in this unholy hot spot that I encouraged the disciples to proclaim who I was. Peter's declaration, "You are the Christ, the Son of the living God," echoed and rang throughout the same location as the worship of the false gods! I used it as an announcement!

Oh, what a triumph that was! And with that, I was throwing down the gauntlet. It was one of those audacious "in-your-face" moments that pricked those fallen princes and powers. I was now blatantly challenging them and their authority *on their own ground.*

It was a challenge they accepted and followed with a plan to kill me.

Mt Hermon had once been known as the mountain of God. It had long been recognized as a place of worship. It was the highest mountain within Israel and was the northern boundary of the land given to Israel and I was already at work reclaiming and taking it back from the evil that had been inhabiting it.

Within that place of worship at the base of the mountain, there were many niches carved into the walls. These were places one could place an idol and make it into a place of worship. These niches were known as "gates."

Now that you know this, perhaps my words will take on a new meaning. Do you recall what I said to Simon? – That's when I first called him "Peter" and said that I will build my church and the "gates of hell" shall not prevail against it (Matthew 16:18).

Do you see now what I was doing? I was at the geographical base of false worship. I was issuing a proclamation that I was preparing to take back the authority that had been given to "gods" over the nations. I would use what they abused. At one time they had been given dominion and guardianship over the nations, and this was my public service announcement that change was coming!

Yes, I was baiting and provoking the false gods and spiritual powers inhabiting this place all those who accepted worship from the people. And it was here... at this place... and at this time that the spiritual war between Me and the evil powers was taken to a new level. You might call it "DEFCON 1", and with that, I provoked them – and I meant to. Why?

Because they needed a reason, a provoking, to find a plan to kill me. For me to fulfill my reason and purpose, I needed to die for the sins of the world. And it was from this time that I began to show my disciples that I must die and suffer many things of the elders and chief priests and scribes and be killed, and after three days rise again (Matthew 16:21).

I fully understood what was about to happen. It had to happen. It was the only way to fulfill all the prophecy about the Messiah and to complete the plan my Father and I set in motion for the salvation of mankind.

Of course, Peter immediately wanted to chastise me and began to rebuke me, telling me how such a thing should not happen. But he simply didn't have the insight to the plan the Godhead had chosen before the world was created (Matthew 16:22).

After having been recently congratulated that his thoughts had come from the Father, Peter didn't now recognize that his current thinking came from a different and outside source. He was so surprised when I turned and told him his current thinking was from Satan! I even made it personal by looking him in the eyes and saying, "Get thee behind me, Satan!" He got the message (Matthew 16:23).

What I was trying to explain to him was that while his thinking appeals to earthly thinking, it was a stumbling block that would keep me from going where I needed to go and doing what I needed to do. How long does it take to go from thinking spiritual thoughts to evil ones? - Peter learned that it could happen in an instant. His idea was obstructing my path to where the Father was taking me. He just didn't see all that God saw.

And neither did the principalities, powers, rulers of darkness, that is, the gods of this age. But, Paul fully captured this idea when he wrote:

"We do, however, speak a message of wisdom among
the mature, but not the wisdom of this age or of the
rulers of this age, who are coming to nothing. No,
we declare God's wisdom, a mystery that has been
hidden and that God destined for our glory before
time began. None of the rulers of this age understood
it, for if they had, they would not have crucified the
Lord of glory."

(1 Corinthians 2:6-8; NIV)

Paul was trying to explain to you that there are two ways of
looking at these events. You can look at them through the eyes of a
man, or through the eyes of a mature believer who sees and under-
stands both the plans and the ways of God.

It's not always easy to do. That's what Solomon recognized when
I taught him that there is a way that *seems* right to a man, but it
ends in death (Proverbs 14:12).

My Father said the same thing, just with different words. He
put it this way:

"For my thoughts are not your thoughts, nor are your
ways, My ways."

(Isaiah 55:8-9)

It's safe to say that the powers and authorities, the "gods" of this
age, had no idea they were playing right into the plan the Father,
Holy Spirit and I crafted before we created anything at all. They
could only respond to my words and my proclamation with the idea
of killing me to keep me from fulfilling my role. They thought they
had to kill me to stop God's plan of overthrowing them.

Of course, they had tried to kill me previously, but to no avail, for my time had not yet come (John 7:30), but this time was not like the previous attempts. This time, the timing was right.

I was battling on two fronts now: one was with the enemy and the other was with friends. The disciples were quite unsettled to hear of my coming death. So, it was from that time on that I began to teach them that all these things must happen... that I would suffer, die and rise again. Even then, it was with limited success, and they didn't come to grips with the reality of it all until my resurrection.

Little did the rulers of this age know that by killing Me, they sealed their own doom. They sealed the salvation plan for mankind and could not prevent all authority being transferred to Me after my resurrection. As Paul said, if they had known what they were doing, they wouldn't have sought to kill me (1 Corinthian 2:8).

Let me give you two special insights while we're still on this subject of Mt Hermon.

First, when I told the disciples that if their faith was only as small as a mustard seed, they could say to this mountain, "Be moved from here to there" and it would move, I was speaking about two different things. Of course, I was speaking in hyperbole about the mountain itself, but I was also speaking about religious workers.

Let me explain.

When you say a subject is "heavy", one of the things you mean is that it's important and serious, big or complex. The people in my day on earth used similar wordplay. When something was big, serious, and important, they called it a "mountain." The important leaders, like the Sanhedrin, the Pharisees and the Sadducees were known as "mountains." So, yes, I was speaking in exaggeration of Mt

Hermon, but also of the religious leaders who had been stumbling blocks to my ministry.

Secondly, if you recall, it was shortly after that, that I brought Peter, James and John up to a high mountain and I allowed myself to be transfigured. My face shone like the sun and my clothes became as white as the light. That was also the time when Moses and Elijah appeared with me. And my glory began to shine through the mere human shell that covered my being (Matthew 17:1).

So, to what mountain do you think I took them? I strategically chose this place, Mt Hermon, to further provoke and challenge the demonic and unholy ones in that area.

You see, I chose the enemy's home base to antagonize them. Why? I wanted to "poke the bear." I needed to prod, goad and provoke them to bring about my death and to do it now.

It was at this time that my Father confirmed Me as His Son. The disciples needed to hear it and the demons did too. It was just one more step in affirming that I would now be targeted and that this was not a case of mistaken identity (Matthew 17:5).

Adam, are you now starting to see how the giants of the Old Testament and the locations of the New Testament begin to mingle and mesh? Bashan, Mt Hermon, the gods, the fallen angels, their unholy headquarters and base, the place of my declaration as the Son of God... all these things were happening when and where they did – for a purpose.

Now, let me tackle another part of your question. Why were the giants a big deal in the way I have spoken of them? Adam, you need to understand that when I took on the incarnation, that is, when I was born and came to mankind in the flesh, I came with a specific purpose. I came to be born among you, live just as you do, but without sin. I was to be the perfect man. That's exactly how Luke tried to present me in his gospel account.

To be the perfect man and to live as one of you – there had to be a direct and pure lineage from the original Adam to me. There could be no tainting and no sin. It had to be this way for me to be the perfect sacrifice suitable to appease the Father's anger against mankind's sin. Remember, purity is one of the ingredients in my "Jesus Box."

The mixing of the angels and humans produced an unclean, unholy mix and it was within the plans of Satan and his angels to pollute the genetic code of mankind. By doing so, they would have corrupted my own genealogy. They wanted to bring pollution into my lineage and thereby poison my acceptability as a pure sacrifice for mankind's sin. It was a diabolical plan that had eternal and infinite consequences.

The battle was heating up and was taking place menacingly over that mountain. It should be no surprise that to this day the dust has not yet settled. It is certain that "the battle rages on…"

Provokingly yours,

—Jesus

9

Demons

Dear Jesus,

Thanks so much for bringing more clarification to the topic of those giants. I had no idea that there was a connection between the giant King Og of Bashan and the "what and why" you were teaching the disciples at Mount Hermon.

I really want to ask about a topic that we haven't touched on, and that's the topic of demons. They were hardly mentioned in the Old Testament, but they seem to be abundant in the New Testament.

They don't seem as powerful as the Principalities and Powers, but they do show up a lot and resist your work. Are demons just less authoritative fallen angels?

Some demonic effects sound a great deal like mental health problems. Are they related?

Is humanity still plagued with demons today?

They seemed to be readily accepted in biblical times but hardly seem active today. Why?

Still posing questions,

—Adam

Dear Adam,

You are maturing in your knowledge of the spiritual world and I'm always happy to answer your questions. I'm glad your thirst for knowing is such a part of your life. It's quite timely that you asked this question right after learning about the giants, for you see, the giants had a lot to do with the demons, but I will get to that later.

You are correct, dealing with demons was a major factor in both, identifying me and in establishing my kingdom. In fact, my authority over the demons was one of the identifying traits I sent to John the Baptizer when he needed a confirmation that I was the Messiah (Luke 7:19-21).

You were correct in your statement that demons are lesser spiritual beings and that's a good way to put it. They are spirits and therefore, they don't have temporal, physical bodies. You don't see demons and their pictures aren't cataloged on spiritual wanted posters.

Demons do have abilities: strength, knowledge and evil intentions. Being spirits without bodies, they do look for opportunities to take on a bodily form. But, unlike angels, they can't take on that form on their own. They are not ministering spirits to My elect people; they are malevolent interfering spirits without bodies that desire interaction in your world.

At one time, they did have a body to dwell in, but now without one, they seek means of both, entering your physical world and to bring distress with them. Think about it, you never read of a "good" demon that brought "Good" into the world.

I hope you remember how I defined "gods." They are *person*-alities, they are beings that are superior in power, knowledge, authority and are of a higher level of creation than humanity. People seek their favor through offerings, sacrifices, loyalty and more. They offer these gods what they have in hopes of attaining what they do not have.

This is what I meant when I told Moses that the people should no longer offer their sacrifices unto devils, or demons, with whom they used to seek favor (Leviticus 17:7).

And it's what I meant when instructing Paul that what the pagans offer in sacrifices, they were offering to demons, and I wanted you to have no part in that (1 Corinthians 10:20).

Demons may also be associated with "familiar spirits." These are spirits that are welcomed by a person to obtain knowledge beyond normal means. I had a lot to say about them too.

I gave strong warnings and instructions as far back as in Moses' day. I said,

Consulting such spirits is so acrimonious to me that it is one of the several reasons I took King Saul's throne from him… and his life too (1 Chronicles 10:13-14).

I warned the saints through the words of John that they should not trust, or believe, every spirit. They were to test the spirits to see if they were from me (1 John 4:1-3). And, Adam, those same guidelines apply to you. Just because you live much later than them, and just because you live in a day of technology, that doesn't exclude you or make you immune to them.

I even urged Luke to give you a real-life example of such a person. So, he wrote of the time he and Paul were going to prayer and they encountered a slave girl who had a spirit of divination. What she prophesied was true, but the spirit was not of me. Paul got so annoyed with her daily demonstrations he took authority of the situation and commanded the demon to leave her (Acts 16:16-19).

When I commanded Moses to give both, warnings and penalties for seeking guidance from fortune-tellers, sorcerers, charmers, mediums, necromancers or one who inquires of the dead, I was deadly serious (Deuteronomy 18:10). These spirits and those who seek them are an abomination to me. Those who seek "good" from any source other than me are going to be disappointed.

How I wish people would just seek me and all these things that are necessary, helpful and good will be added to them. They worry about what they will eat, what they will wear and what they will have. I've demonstrated to them that the birds of the air and the lilies of the fields are not worried, but I take care of them. How much more will I take care of those who love me and seek me. Seeking it, as they will, they can't add a single hour to their lifetime. Don't they understand that I clothe the grass of the field that is alive today and gone tomorrow, how much more will I share "Good" to them? All they must do is seek Me first (Matthew 6:25-30).

These demons do have knowledge, and they do have authority, but their abilities are quite limited. No wise men, enchanters, magicians or astrologers can show mysteries and answers that I do not supply (Daniel 2:27). And strength? Oh yes, they are strong beyond your imagination.

Spirits can bring immense power. Do you remember Samson? If you recall, his strength was only present when My spirit would come upon him (Judges 14:6, 19, 15:14).

The evil spirits bring the same. How about the man who lived in the graveyard and was possessed by demons? Do you recall how the villagers tried to tie him down with ropes and chains and yet, he broke through the bindings (Mark 5:1-13)?

And let's not forget about those sons of Sceva who wanted to brag about casting out demons until they found one who did not recognize them. While I had given my disciples authority over demons (Mark 3:15), these sons of Sceva were imitators, cheap copies, of my real disciples. While they may have said the right words, there was no authority in them over the demons. The demons recognized that and instead of obeying these sons, they jumped on them, beat them up and sent them running off, hopefully, having learned a lesson (Acts 19:11-16).

Adam, if you remember all these occasions and my thoughts on them, let's deal with the question of where these demons came from and how they operate.

I told you earlier that your question of giants had links to understanding the demons. As you recall, the giants were the offspring of spiritual beings and human beings. That union brought about a being that was part human and part spirit in nature. When the giants died, like everyone else their bodies were corrupted, decayed and went into the ground. But the spirit within them lived on and once again wanted to enjoy the fruit of the fleshly life, so they sought host bodies in which they could reside… even detestable ones.

I recall how on one occasion I encountered a man who was thoroughly vexed with a legion of spirits. Those spirits recognized me and were afraid that I was there to bring about their final judgment. They begged me to allow them to inhabit the bodies of the unclean pigs rather than face that judgment. I allowed it and when they went into the pigs, the pigs became so distraught they ran off a cliff and perished (Matthew 8:32.)

Oh, their final judgment day will certainly come, just as it will for all those who seek their "good" from a source other than me.

If spirits can come, they can also go. And that's the authority I bequeathed to my disciples, to make the spirits leave. Let me remind you of David, long before he was King. I placed him in the palace of King Saul as a musician; David would often show his skill with the harp. Because of Saul's multiple failures to follow my instructions and because he despised my words, he was often oppressed by a spirit. But it was David's music that was the means to alleviate the effects of those spirits.

As I taught you previously, I allow people to make decisions, but they also must bear the consequences of those decisions. Saul's failure to follow Me resulted in my allowance of an evil spirit to bring him to distress. But David following my heart could relieve that pressure with his music. Time and time again I would encourage Saul to follow Me, and I could show him what relief from that would look like. But time and time again he refused (1 Samuel 18:10-11).

I've given you a lot to think about. Let's review it before I close this letter:

- There are spiritual beings called demons;
- In spiritual hierarchy, they are among those lesser beings;
- They are the spirits left behind from the giants who were the result of the union of spiritual beings and human beings;
- They have knowledge, power and some authority, but are subject to the authority of God;
- There are many instances throughout your Bible of their activities, desires and behavior;
- While powerful, knowledgeable and spiritual, they are limited in their ability and authority;
- The day is coming when they, along with all the other evil entities, will face their final judgment.
- And don't forget, I'm still in control and none of these things surprise me.

Oh, one more thing, Adam. Yes, the effects of an evil spirit within, or upon, a person can look very much like a mental or physical health issue. That's why I warned the church to test the spirits to see if they are of God.

Health issues could be of God in the form of testing or punishment. However, they might also be nothing more than the effects of natural bodily infirmities. Have a headache? Take a pill, listen to relaxing music and check in with God to see if He is trying to get your attention.

But they could be from an evil source. Evil spirits are still often talked about and dealt with in many cultures. However, much of your own culture looks down on those who do and consider themselves *enlightened* and free from such superstition.

However, if you were able to peek behind the hospitals and doctor's office doors you would find that many who suffer still have no relief in spite of all the technology, medicines and remedies available. Rather than choose to believe in a spiritual realm, they just don't understand. Just because you don't talk about demons doesn't mean they are not at work among you.

So, as you can see… "The Battle Rages On."

Discerningly yours,

—Jesus

10

The Devil, He Didn't Make You Do It

Dear Jesus,

I've learned a lot about the spiritual realm and why Satan is our greatest enemy. It was he that deceived and tempted Eve first, and then the original Adam – and he continues, hoping to set his throne above yours. I also understand that even if he realizes he can't pull off the cosmic coup, he desires to drag us down with him. I understand that to this day, and on until judgment day, he will continue his onslaught against us.

So, here is my question: Can Satan make us do things we don't want? And is he to blame for all of our temptations and sins?

I'm curious again,

—Adam

Dear Adam,

As always, it's good to hear from you. I must admit, it's always interesting to see what questions you will ask next and this one is no disappointment. So, yes– let's talk about Satan, his wiles, his ways, his desires and his abilities.

Before we begin, I'm going to keep reminding you of something. You need to keep this in the forefront of your mind. None of this surprises me. Satan's fall was known ahead of time, as was his deception of Eve and Adam. Humanity's fall didn't catch us off-guard. That's why I keep reminding you that my earthly role was planned before the foundations of the world were laid.

Why? Because humanity is worth saving... even if much of it dismisses me or rejects me. The love I share with those who welcome me is worth it.

Having said all that, let's get down to it!

First, let's list the things you know... they will help point you to what you want to know:

- Satan's name is Lucifer, and he was a star among the stars of heaven.
- His pride went beyond who he was – he thought he was more than he was.
- In his pride, he rejected my authority and my plans.
- My plans included the making of mankind, and I would eventually call them "sons of God" just as I had done with the angels.
- I crowned Adam as king on earth, and he was to take responsibility for all that was on the earth. He was to enlarge my garden, take jurisdiction over the earth and all within it.

- Lucifer felt his position was being whittled away with mankind being raised to something close to his own.
- By pride and jealousy, he desired to raise himself higher than he was and sought the Father's throne.
- He sought to bring mankind down. If he was going to fall, he would take mankind with him.
- Besides that, if God had some preference for mankind, then it suited him to spoil that preference showing that mankind can reject Him and fall from Him too.

But now your question touches on the subject of just what can Satan do? How much destruction can he bring? What authority does he have? Can he make you do something you don't want to do?

All these questions will touch on the subject of "How much will YOU be responsible for when judgment day arrives?" Doesn't it?

First, let's give you an accurate picture of a cherub. A cherub is NOT the chubby little figurine with wings, a bow and arrows. That Valentine Day character is non-existent and only lives on in fanciful imaginations and cartoons.

A cherub is among the upper echelons of the spiritual world. It is a celestial winged creature with human, animal, or birdlike characteristics and who functions as a throne-bearer of God. He is truly a formidable, fearful, magnificent and majestic creature.

I've described them in greater detail in your Bible. There, I let Ezekiel describe them:

> "And from the midst of it came the likeness of four living creatures. And this was their appearance: they had a human likeness, but each had four faces, and each of them had four wings. Their legs were straight,

and the soles of their feet were like the sole of a calf's foot. And they sparkled like burnished bronze. Under their wings on their four sides they had human hands. And the four had their faces and their wings thus: their wings touched one another. Each one of them went straight forward, without turning as they went. As for the likeness of their faces, each had a human face. The four had the face of a lion on the right side, the four had the face of an ox on the left side, and the four had the face of an eagle. Such were their faces. And their wings were spread out above. Each creature had two wings, each of which touched the wing of another, while two covered their bodies. And each went straight forward. Wherever the spirit would go, they went, without turning as they went. As for the likeness of the living creatures, their appearance was like burning coals of fire, like the appearance of torches moving to and fro among the living creatures. And the fire was bright, and out of the fire went forth lightning. And the living creatures darted to and fro, like the appearance of a flash of lightning. Now as I looked at the living creatures, I saw a wheel on the earth beside the living creatures, one for each of the four of them. As for the appearance of the wheels and their construction: their appearance was like the gleaming of beryl. And the four had the same likeness, their appearance and construction being as if it were a wheel within a wheel. When they went, they went in any of their four directions without turning as they went. And their rims were tall and awesome, and the rims of all four were full of eyes all around.

And when the living creatures went, the wheels went beside them; and when the living creatures rose from the earth, the wheels rose. Wherever the spirit wanted to go, they went, and the wheels rose along with them, for the spirit of the living creatures was in the wheels. When those went, these went; and when those stood, these stood; and when those rose from the earth, the wheels rose along with them, for the spirit of the living creatures was in the wheels.

Over the heads of the living creatures there was the likeness of an expanse, shining like awe-inspiring crystal, spread out above their heads. And under the expanse their wings were stretched out straight, one toward another. And each creature had two wings covering its body. And when they went, I heard the sound of their wings like the sound of many waters, like the sound of the Almighty, a sound of tumult like the sound of an army. When they stood still, they let down their wings."

—*Ezekiel 1:5-22 (ESV)*

Yes, these are fearsome creatures with greater power, authority and strength than your Valentine's Day pictures – and probably more than you ever dared to imagine!

Not only were they guardians for God's throne, but they were also depicted on top of the Ark of the Covenant... yes, the ark portrayed in the Indiana Jones movie, the one created in Moses' day, the same one that King David had transported to Jerusalem to be placed in God's temple. They were embroidered into the veil that divided the Holy place and from the Holy of Holies within the temple and one even stood with a flaming sword to keep mankind from entering back into Eden, the Garden of God, and eating from the Tree of Life.

A cherub is no push-over being who can be argued with, aligned with, threatened or coerced. This is a fierce, frightful, supernatural, divine being. They are not to be trifled with, not even by other high-ranking angels. Do you remember how Jude mentioned that even Michael, an archangel, did not presume to level an accusation against the devil when contending with him about the body of Moses (Jude 1:8-9).

Notice too, that Lucifer was *the* anointed cherub... not your run-of-the-mill, ordinary fierce creature. He was selected, appointed and set aside as one that was special, privileged and distinct from all others. Let's look at how I described him in even greater detail.

"You were the signet of perfection,

full of wisdom and perfect in beauty.

You were in Eden, the garden of God;

every precious stone was your covering,

sardius, topaz, and diamond,

beryl, onyx, and jasper,

sapphire, emerald, and carbuncle;

and crafted in gold were your settings

and your engravings.

On the day that you were created

they were prepared.

You were an anointed guardian cherub.

I placed you; you were on the holy mountain of God;

in the midst of the stones of fire you walked.

You were blameless in your ways

from the day you were created,

till unrighteousness (iniquity) was found in you."

—Ezekiel 18:12-15 (ESV)

Due to his abundant glory, he began to think too much of himself and decided that it would be better to rule than to serve. His pride got in the way of his holiness and devotion to God. His heart was proud because of his beauty; he corrupted his wisdom for the sake of his splendor (Ezekiel 28:17).

Glorious? Oh yes! And there is nothing in your Bible that says this changed when he fell from his prominent position. That's why I warned that Satan can disguise himself as an angel of light (2 Corinthians 11:14).

You see, Adam, although his character and passions changed, he is still beautiful, but he comes only to steal and kill and to destroy (John 10:10).

And I assure you, he is here to steal you from God, kill your eternal life and destroy your dreams and your destiny of being and doing all God created you to be.

Now, let's go to the poignant question… "Can he make you sin?" The short answer is "No."

But there are other things to consider – like humanity's own nature. I urged John to warn you about this factor. I told him that all that is in the world, the lust of the flesh, and the lust of the eyes, and the pride of life… these things are not of the Father, but of the world (1 John 2:16).

And I gave words to James too. I told him that every man is tempted, when he is drawn away of his own lust, and enticed to sin. Satan doesn't "make" you sin… you choose to do it when led away by your own lust. I went on to say that when lust has conceived, it brings forth sin... and when sin is finished it ends in death (James 1:14).

As you can see, you are much of the source of your own sin... it wasn't him!

You do evil because you choose to do so.

You lie because you choose to do so.

You covet because you allow your eyes to linger on what you want.

You lust because of your own nature seeing who, or what, you wanted.

When you are enticed and sin, during the normal circumstances of life, it's because you wanted to. It's just that Satan knows how to bring that temptation to your attention!

Now, please understand this Adam, it is NOT a sin to be tempted. Even I was tempted by Satan, but I resisted him. Temptation is not a sin. SIN is sin and that is your choice. Sadly, after your namesake, the original Adam sinned, it became a part of your nature to sin, too. That is what is passed down from the beginning generation to every generation of mankind since. That's why I had to say, there are none *good* but the Father.

Adam, yes... be discouraged when you sin, but not when you are tempted. And know this – you have me as your High Priest, who is able to sympathize with your weaknesses, but one who in every respect has been tempted just as you are, yet without sin (Hebrews 4:15). Adam, I know what you're going through. I can relate to it. And I can help you through it.

I want you to understand, you are a sinful creature, but not because of all the sins you commit or omit, but because IT'S YOUR NATURE.

Satan can tempt you.

Satan can entice you.

Satan can deceive you.

But, he can't make you sin.

He will delight in your sin, but he can't make you do it.

Did you ever hear the story of a farmer who saw a young boy sitting on a fence by the farmer's apple tree? The farmer approached the boy and asked, "Are you trying to steal my apples?" and the boy responded, "No sir, I'm trying *NOT* to!"

You've been told to "resist temptation and flee from the devil," but let me tell you something even better: "Resist the devil and flee from temptation."

Remember with me when Joseph was being tempted by Potiphar's wife. He didn't stand there trying to resist the temptation to have her. No, he fled so quickly, he even left without his coat. He fled!! (Genesis 39:19-34)

Every indication I could give you in your Bible shows that Satan is waiting and urging you to choose sin. But he doesn't know if you will do it, or not. Even Job's story is one where Job is severely affected by drastic circumstances presented and orchestrated by Satan. Satan watched to see if Job would choose to sin. Job was directly attacked by Satan, but Satan had no power to make him sin... and so it is with you (Job 1:2).

A fish, by its own nature, wants to eat a worm. A fisherman, knowing this, will entice the fish to his hook by baiting him with what his nature desires. The fisherman didn't make the fish bite the hook and the worm didn't make the fish bite the hook. Rather, it bit the hook when it was enticed to eat what its nature desired.

This is a great analogy for you to consider. Satan doesn't make you choose to sin.

And the object of your lust didn't make you choose to sin.

You sinned, because by your nature, you wanted what was being offered. Whether to sin or not, whether to fall for the enticement or not, whether to resist the temptation or not, THAT is a part of the spiritual warfare you've been so inquisitive about. Spiritual warfare includes that, but it is certainly not limited to that.

I remember one of the country-western songs you used to enjoy as it was sung by Kenny Rogers. It was entitled, "The Gambler" and it was about an old-time gambler giving advice to a younger man about the trade he was embarking on. In his wisdom, the old man talked about the cards and the young man himself...

You gotta know when to hold 'em, know when to fold 'em

Know when to walk away and know when to run.

My advice has always been similar – flee temptation. As long as you are alive, the old nature is with you and it will be tempted. And THAT is why... "The Battle Rages On..."

Untemptingly yours,

—Jesus

11

Heaven and Earth

Dear Adam,

I'm going to take the lead and preempt your questions on a new topic. It's not something you've written about, but I want to go ahead and explain some things you need to know. Doing this will broaden your view and help you comprehend the scope of our current talks on spiritual warfare.

The topic I want to step into has to do with the mysterious relationship you find between heaven and earth. Why? Because there is one - and far too often humanity seems blinded to it. Let me say it up front – heaven and earth *are* connected.

Sometimes they have a cause-and-effect relationship. That is, what happens in one place affects the other place. What happens in one location can bring about a response in the other.

For instance, remember the Divine Council meeting we discussed previously… the one when a decision was being made about how to handle King Ahab? What he was doing demanded a response. I witnessed the events in heaven, called a council meeting, a decision was made and then judgment was carried out on earth.

On an earlier occasion, Cain killed his brother Abel and shortly thereafter, the voice of Abel's blood cried out unto me from the ground and I heard it in heaven. Events that "ring" on earth can "gong" in heaven! A whisper here can be a shout there.

I'm not telling you something you don't know – I'm just re-inforcing what you do know and enlarging your vision of what's happening. Isn't this the basis of your prayers? On earth, you pray. In heaven, I hear. And, in heaven, I act. On earth, there is a response.

This is what my people have always hoped for. It was Solomon who pleaded that I would hear in heaven the words of repentance of his people. I remember him beseeching and imploring over and over again that I would hear from heaven and act... hear from heaven and forgive... hear from heaven and judge... it was all written down for you to read in 2 Chronicles 6.

When people brought sacrifices to the tabernacle or the temple, it was with an intent and expectation, that I would respond from heaven. When Israel went astray, I corrected them. When they wandered, I gathered them. And, when they repented, I forgave. Yes, heaven and earth are intricately intertwined.

But Adam, there's a lot more to it than that. There are sounds you don't hear, activities you don't see and events you can't imagine, even though they surround you. Do you recall the episode in Elisha's life when the plains were inundated with the enemy? If you had been there, you would have seen the surprise – and the fear – in his servant's face when he saw the multitude of enemies.

Yes, the servant got up early in the morning to take care of his chores, but when he went outside he was astonished at the expanse of the enemy's army. There were troops, horses and chariots everywhere. Elisha had the wherewithal to calm him and then he asked me to open the eyes of the servant to see the unseen. That's when I responded from heaven and I opened the man's eyes and he saw that the hillside was filled with, not only horses, but chariots of fire!

I want you to fully understand, Adam, when I work from heaven and things move on earth – you may be like the servant and just not be able to see what is happening beside you, before you and after you.

But even that is not all that is happening. There is so much more going on around you and you don't even feel a breeze from its passing by. You wonder why I'm silent after you pray and why I don't hear when you call – but I do. The enemy has armies too – and they do not stand idly by while mine work for my kingdom. They will try to intercept, interfere and interrupt my kingdom's work.

We could chat about Daniel and the time he prayed from earth, and I heard in heaven... AND I sent an immediate reply. However, my messenger to Daniel was waylaid by other spiritual authorities. The prince of Persia withstood my angel. I had to send Michael, one of the chief princes to free him up and finally get the message to Daniel, but it took 3 weeks (Daniel 10).

Life in your world is constant and full of activity... and so it is in the unseen realm. There is both action and reaction between your realm and mine, and there is also interaction.

That's why I told my followers to not despise, (or look down on), the children, for their angels in heaven are watching and they see my Father's face (Matthew 18:10-11). Do you think they are watching the child and my Father's face because they have nothing else to do? – No. Action, reaction and interaction is constant.

I recall a bit of action one day... It was after I authorized and sent out my disciples to successfully cast out demons – that I saw Satan fall like lightning from heaven (Luke 10:7).

On another occasion, there was hellacious activity on earth that demanded I reach from heaven and respond. I saw the wickedness of humanity had grown great and evil was continually in their hearts, so I sent a flood in response (Genesis 6).

It was not long after that people rebelled once again and after I instructed them to spread out on the earth, they decided to build a tower and stay together in one place. Because of what was happening here (Earth), I decided there (heaven), to respond and react here (Earth) (Genesis 10).

Adam, search your Bible and you'll find that I usually respond to rebellion, and to my people forsaking me by bringing droughts, plagues, pestilence, wind, fire and floods! I'll use anything I have to, to bring my people back to me. And don't forget WHY I do that. It's not because I'm pouting, I'm not brooding, I'm not seeking vengeance. I WANT THE BEST for them and when they forsake me, they are abandoning their only means of acquiring what they really want and need. Again, this goes back to our discussion about why I am a jealous God.

There is a connection - a link - between heaven and earth. Heaven cares about earth - everything about earth. Remember, I put your namesake, the original Adam, in charge of this place – to groom it and care for it. I haven't abandoned earth or its inhabitants. In fact, if you keep reading your Bible thoroughly, you discover that I never intended mankind to abandon earth either. And that's despite how so many talk about leaving and going to heaven. Didn't you read the last chapters of My book? Neither I, nor you, are forsaking this place. I will re-make it!

Earth will be mankind's final and ultimate abiding place, not heaven.

Look for it in John's book of Revelation. It's there that he tells you plainly that heaven comes down. New Jerusalem will come down out of heaven to the earth. And I will bring my followers with me. I will remake the heavens and the earth.

Yes, yes, yes… There is a strong connection between heaven and earth. Let me say it again, there is action, reaction, interaction between here and there.

You are probably wondering WHY? Why do I care so much? I care because my 'box' is full of "good" And I did it to perpetuate and distribute all that "goodness."

Adam, I created this place. I won't forsake it. It's MINE! It's all mine – and you are too. Yes, I care and interact with all that I made. I made it to enjoy, and I will hold mankind accountable for taking care of it. Let me remind you – all things were made by Me, through Me and for Me!

If I had made it for you, I might take you elsewhere when its usefulness is over. But I made it for me and I will redeem it all.

As a child, if you ever lived in a two-story house and made noise downstairs, you might have heard your parents say, "Don't make me come down there!" That's what my heart has cried out so many times as I've seen mankind hate and watched the desecration of so many parts of your planet, which used to be the abiding place of my garden. That's why I will re-create this place, not forsake it.

There are many more days ahead with even more actions, re-actions and interactions between heaven and earth. The enemy is far from finished with their plans of destruction of all my "good." They will set up their own version of me, an "antichrist," and their own prophet, a false prophet, and their own armies, but it will be their final actions before I bring judgment and set up my kingdom.

At that time, the prayers of untold millions will be answered. For over two thousand years, you've prayed that my will will be done on earth as it is in heaven. That day is posted on my Father's calendar and it is coming!

Truth be told, at that time, I won't come as a baby laid in a manger. It will be like a lion coming to reclaim my throne, my people and my place – and I have to admit, I'm looking forward to it.

Let there be no question about it, that day is coming! But, in the meantime, and as you well know, "The Battle Rages On..."

Jubilantly yours,

—Jesus

12

Defining Our Words

Dear Jesus,

Thanks for taking so much time to help me grow aware and to grow in knowledge of you and all you've done. I do feel that I'm growing exponentially, and I want my maturity to grow with my knowledge. I'm so grateful that you're so easy to approach and you don't mind all my questions.

Having said that, I need to let you know I feel rather inadequate when I pose my questions without great clarity. I see that you seem to use precise words that mean exactly what you want to say. My lack of an adequate vocabulary sometimes jumbles words and meaning so I'm not as accurate in what I'm saying.

For instance, I've read your words like: trespass, sin, iniquity, forsaken and rebellion and I tend to just group them all together under the word "sin." I'd like to be more meaningful and precise when I express my thoughts, but I just don't understand the differences in all these words.

A little help, please?

—Adam

Dear Adam,

I welcome your inquiries... I want you to grow and mature, so I want to be available to you. As for my time? – Well, you could say I have plenty of that! And I'm always happy to share it with you. And I'm always glad to hear you asking for more. I let it be known that any man who lacks wisdom, only needs to ask (James 1:5).

You are correct. I do try to say what I mean and mean what I say, and words are a very special form of communication. No two words mean the same thing, that's why there are different words. So, let's get your words and your meaning to match up... and that will help you understand me better too.

First, let's talk about the word SIN. It's one of the most used words when talking about ungodly things. Most people assume SIN means evil. But that's not as accurate as it could be. SIN is "falling short." Think of an arrow streaking through the air toward its target, but gravity affects it and it falls short of its mark.

I have set a standard of moral perfection. I've described it with words like "pure," "righteous," "without blemish" and so forth. And I've written it out with specific instructions like, "thou shalt" and "thou shalt not." To SIN is to fall short of those instructions and definitions. You aim to hit the mark I've set, but you fall short.

Even the Pharaoh, when confronted by Moses, used this word when describing his actions. He said he had sinned against Me and Moses (Exodus 10:16). And Achan said the same thing when he admitted to taking something he had been told not to take (Joshua 7:20). It's the same word used by Israel when they repented and admitted they had sinned against me (Judges 10:10). And it was used by Jeremiah as he described the admission of guilt by the people. They confessed,

"We have sinned against the Lord, our God. We and our fathers, from our youth, even unto this day, we have not obeyed the voice of the Lord, our God."

—Jeremiah 3:25 (ESV)

Let's distinguish SIN from TRESPASS. When you sin, you fall short of the target, but when you trespass, you are stepping across a line. Trespass is a type, or kind, of sin. Think about the last time you went for a walk in the woods, and you came to a fence with a "No Trespassing" sign attached to it. You immediately knew that this fence was a line you should not cross.

In a similar way, when you trespass against me, what should come to your mind is that I made a rule and drew a moral line that said, "Do not cross this line." When you recognize the line, but step across it anyway – well, that's a trespass.

When Abigail was pleading with David to forgive someone, she asked David to please forgive the "trespass." Someone had stepped across a line David had made (1 Samuel 25:28).

Paul used the same word when describing Adam's initial sin. I had set a defining line – "Don't eat of this one tree," but Adam did. So, Adam's sin (falling short of moral perfection) was a "trespass" (Romans 5:15).

So, to help clarify – All trespassing against God is a sin, but not all sin is a trespass. SIN is the large umbrella of falling short, that is more specifically described by various types of sin.

Now, let's talk about INIQUITY. Iniquity is the dirtiness that is alive and well within you. It is more associated with the condition of a heart than the action of the person. For instance, I spoke about the heart condition of the Amorite people to Abram. I was explaining to him why he could not yet have the land of the Amorite people, in spite of all their sin.

As I bring you into my confidence, let me explain that I set the boundaries of all the peoples and nations. Kings and princes may think their principalities are theirs and that which belongs to others is available for the taking, but it is me that sets the boundaries.

Back when I gave authority to the Watchers to care for the various nations, I not only assigned the Watchers to the nations, but I assigned borders for those nations (Deuteronomy 32:8). Abram needed to know it was not yet time for Me to give him the land I promised. The Amorites were still in that land and their *iniquity* was not yet full (Genesis 15:16). The condition of their evil hearts had not yet reached the point of no return.

This is the word Moses chose when he was describing the heart condition of the Israelites and how I had been patient with them. He said I was a God of steadfast love, merciful, gracious, slow to anger and one who forgives their INIQUITY (Exodus 34:6).

Even when I used a form of this word when I described Nathaniel, I said he was a man with no "guile" – that is, his heart was in good shape and not formed by iniquity (John 1:47).

In our conversations so far, you've noticed I used the word REBELLION extensively, when describing the actions of some of the fallen angels. Again, rebellion is sin, but not all sin is rebellion.

REBELLION is an act of resistance to an existing authority. As you are aware, I am the ultimate authority. I had all authority in the beginning, delegated much to certain angels and then I reclaimed it after my resurrection. I spoke openly about it and reassured my disciples by telling them, *all* authority in both, heaven and earth, were mine. (Matthew 28:18).

Resistance to my authority is rebellion. Now, let's put all these words together to make even more sense of them.

A person that falls short of moral perfection is one in sin.

A sinful heart's desire and nature is iniquity.

One's iniquity may embolden one to trespass.

When one resists my authority, it is rebellion.

I hope this is starting to make sense. Let's do the same thing and talk about words that lend towards righteousness. In fact, why don't we start with that one?

RIGHTEOUS, or righteousness, is a heart that does "Good", or what is right. Get that connection between *right* and *right*-eousness? After Adam's initial sin, there were none that were righteous. Paul described it something it like this, there are none that are righteous, no not one (Romans 3:10).

He went on to say that those whose heart desires "Good," the righteous shall live by faith (Romans 1:16). He also spoke of My right heart when he used the phrase, "the righteousness of God" (Romans 1:7). And he also talked about my judgment upon sin and sinners as being done with a right heart, or with "righteous judgment" (Romans 2:1).

I need humanity to understand that while most of them see themselves as not being too bad or too evil – they don't measure them-selves by my standards. There are NONE that are righteous – no not one. With that in mind, they should be asking the question: "If we don't have any righteousness – how can we get it?" And that is both a great question and an important one.

To be worthy of heaven and being a part of my kingdom, you must be righteous… you must have a right heart. But you don't and you can't make one. If you desire it, you must obtain it from Me. I have it – I have a righteous heart so big I can share it with you.

King David understood this and wrote, "Create in me a clean heart and renew a right spirit within me." (Psalm 51:10)

Again, Paul was trying to help my followers understand this. Paul aptly said that My righteousness, the righteousness of God was made known, not by the giving of laws that no one could fully obey, but it is a gift given by me to those who will have faith in me (Romans 3:21). It's required to enter into heaven, and it brings new life to a person (Romans 1:17).

You see, when someone places their faith in Me, I take that very seriously and something astounding happens. By putting their faith in me, they are loyally aligning themselves with me and my standards. The righteousness I have I will give to them so they can stand confidently before God the Father when final and ultimate judgement begins.

Paul tried, he really tried hard, to be good enough to stand before me, but he knew he wasn't. He tried to keep the laws and the moral perfection, but nobody is good enough to do that. He then described himself and his position by saying, everything he had worked for in getting to God was of no use. He counted all that he had done as a loss, and he quit depending on his works so that he could depend on nothing less than me. He began to seek me... he treasured what I had to offer and he finally gained me and my righteousness (Philippians 3:9).

Let me give you just a few more words that I think will help guide your thoughts in the days ahead. Let's try three more words that are often used when describing what I have to give.

JUSTICE. Justice is what people want. When they have been wronged, they want someone to make things right. They seek "justice." When Abraham pleaded with me to not fully destroy Sodom and Gomorrah, he remonstrated that I should be a God who is just. And I was. I am a just God and I did destroy those twin cities, but it wasn't because I wasn't just – it was because I was.

Justice produces judgement that is deserved. There is no vengeance involved: it is the right punishment for the crime. No family that experienced the murder of a loved one wants to see the murderer get off with a slap on the wrist. They want the punishment to be equal to the crime. Look carefully at John's visions in the book of Revelation and when judgement day arrives and the wicked are sentenced, you won't read of anyone complaining and saying, "I don't deserve that."

But, JUSTICE differs from MERCY. If justice is getting what one deserves, MERCY is not getting ALL that they deserve. This is when you may hear a criminal pleading with a judge to extend the mercy of the court when sentencing is near.

GRACE differs from both JUSTICE and MERCY. If Justice is getting what one deserves and Mercy is not getting ALL that one deserves, then GRACE is getting "goodness" when you don't deserve it at all.

Adam, I am a Just God. I am a Merciful God. And I am a God of Grace.

Now, as I close out this letter, let me encourage you to ask "WHY?" Go ahead, Adam, think about it. Why would I be a God who is all three: Just, Merciful, and Gracious?

As you ponder this, let your mind run back to my most fundamental teaching in these letters. I didn't have to create anything or anyone. But, because there is so much 'Good' in me, I wanted to multiply it exponentially. Good wants more good. In choosing to multiply that goodness, I allowed both, angels and humanity, to make choices. They could choose to want me, or not. Both choices have ramifications and consequences.

But, by allowing those choices, and allowing humanity to choose me, I can express my Goodness by being Just with those who rebel against it and giving Mercy and Grace to those who want to partake of that Goodness.

Finally, this is why I told Paul to write to you some guidelines about how to live in your daily life. I told him that whatever is true, whatever is honest, whatever is just, pure and lovely... whatever is of a good report... if there is any virtue, if there is any praise... then, think on these things (Philippians 4:8).

Now, let me encourage you with that as I sign off... think on these things. Think on them when your days are good. Think on them even more when you're having a bad day. You'll need it because The Battle Rages On...

Mercifully yours,

—Jesus

13

Magic vs Miracles

Dear Jesus,

I know this question may sound a little offbeat, but it's a question that has bothered me and I know you can bring clarity to my mind. It's magic. I've found that, when the topic of religion comes up, it seems like a lot of people talk about magic and how they use it.

When I say magic, I don't mean the tricksters and illusionists performing on a stage, but *real* magic. If there is real magic, where does it come from, and how does it work? If it *is* real, are there different kinds of magic, like black magic and white magic?

I know the Bible takes a dim view of magic, but if it isn't real, what's the big deal? And, if it is and if it works, what's the problem?

—*Adam*

Dear Adam

PRESTO! – Here's your answer. (Sorry, I couldn't resist that little introduction to your question). There is a lot to answer here, and you are correct, I did instruct my writers of the Bible to have quite a bit to say about it. I gave quite a few instances of what you call "magic" in the scriptures, and your question does have a lot to do with the spiritual world and spiritual warfare. Before beginning, let me say that this has nothing to do with stage performers. What they do are clever tricks and there's nothing wrong with that. It's sleight-of-hand, or genius gadgets and devices that appear to be magical, but it is nothing more than an illusion. They trick your mind. Think about the very name they give these acts – they are "magic tricks." Tricks are not magic, they are deceptive to your understanding, but any stage magician could show you how his trick is done and with practice you could do it too. Again, stage show 'magic' isn't magic, but it can be a lot of fun and a great source of enjoyment as your mind tries to understand how they 'tricked' you. Once you understand how the trick is done, your mind ceases to be amazed and the marvel of it all disappears. Entertaining? – Yes. Evil? – No.

But, more to the point, is there a real magic? I think the best way to convey this to you is to answer both, "yes" and "no." I know that answer is perplexing, so let me explain. First, let's work with a definition of "magic".

Magic is the power of influencing people, things or the course of events by using a supernatural power.

Now, take a close look at the words in that definition and you'll find two key components:

Power and Supernatural power. That is what brings real magic into our current discussions. Magic is calling upon a source of power that is not from me. It is apart from me, and it is from a source other than me.

You know from our previous discussions how I feel about searching for, yearning for and seeking a power other than me. This goes right back to the heart of why I am a jealous God. When searching for power, or benefits that bring *good* to your situation or life – there is nothing "*gooder*" than me. (Yes, I'll say it again – that's very poor grammar, but it's good theology.)

What you desire in life is what I desire for you – Goodness, that which is Best, Pure, Lovely, True, and all the other ingredients in my Jesus box. Are there other sources of power? Absolutely, that's why I describe them as Principalities, Powers, Rulers of darkness and Spiritual wickedness in HIGH places. These are beings from the spiritual realm who wrap their wickedness to deceive you. They disguise themselves as something desirable and good, but they are not. They want you to open their box which is filled only with what is malevolent.

Please understand, I'm not trying to keep good stuff from you – I'm trying to pave a path that leads you to experience the very best. To do that, I put up guard rails to keep you on the "good" path. I express warnings and give you plenty of examples throughout your Bible.

With that said, I'm going to rehearse some of those for you, so you fully grasp what is happening and why I prohibit "magic".

Let's start with the time I sent Moses before the Pharaoh. Do you remember the episode of him standing before the leader of Egypt, throwing down his staff and it turning into a serpent? I had told Moses and Aaron to work miraculous signs before him and this was the beginning.

Now, let me explain the word I just used – "miraculous." A miracle is when I override or go around the natural laws of your physical world. When I created your world, I did it by setting many natural laws in effect. There are laws of gravity, laws of magnetism and more. What I mean by that is that there are principles I built into creation that make these things work naturally… all the time. A miracle is when I work outside the usual laws to accomplish what I desire. Magic might be deemed the same thing, but it is someone else working outside the usual laws of nature. Notice, I said "someone", there is a power and a source of the power behind the event. These are not *tricks*.

When I wrote to you previously, I never denied that fallen angels are of a higher order of creation, that they have heavenly knowledge, they have higher authority and greater powers than you. They are not limitless, and I have set boundaries, but that doesn't diminish what power, authority and knowledge they do have.

Magic then, is the calling upon them to engage with your world to bring about some effect that would be beneficial to you.

Having understood that, let's go back to our story of Moses. I told Moses and Aaron to take their wooden staff and throw it down before Pharaoh and it would become a serpent. While Moses was prepared and did that, he was not prepared for what followed. The Pharaoh then called his "sorcerers" or magicians; they came with their secret arts (knowledge and power from a source other than God) and did the same. They threw down their staffs and they became serpents, too.

But both the magicians and the Pharaoh were amazed when Moses' staff-serpent swallowed up their staffs (Exodus 7:9-12). In fact, I think both Moses and Aaron were a bit startled by this too.

Let me explain why I did all this. When you read this story in your Bible, you need to understand that I was almost "unknown" in the world. I had placed the Israelites (there were only about 75 of them) into safe keeping in Egypt. There, they would be protected from the marauding and the raiding of potential enemies. They would have food, a safe haven and while in Egypt, they would multiply exponentially.

Yes, it was filled with the worship of many of the fallen angels who had become the gods of the land, but I gave the Israelites the land (suburb) of Goshen as a place to live rather than in the worship center of the city. Neither the Israelites, nor the Egyptians knew Me, but I was about to begin my great publicity campaign to declare who I am.

When I sent Moses and Aaron to the leader of this powerful nation, I knew there would be a series of contests coming and I was going to overcome the power of their gods to make myself famous. This was not because I was on an ego-trip, it was to establish the nation of Israel and show myself as the God of all gods... SO THAT, people would learn to call upon me and seek me from the very source of all that is good.

The Pharaoh, rather than believe in this new God he was hearing about, hardened his heart against me. He refused to believe that I was more powerful than the gods he had come to know. I knew that would be his reaction and so I then used the hardness of his heart to show my greatness and authority over all other gods.

Time and time again, I provoked him through the several miracles Moses brought before him – you know them as the 10 plagues. You'll remember a number of those – the turning of the Nile River into blood, the pestilences of frogs, gnats, flies, hail, and more. Then,

I saved the most devastating for last – the death of the first-born throughout the land.

With that devastating blow, the Pharaoh got my message and allowed my people to leave Egypt, and I was made famous, not only to Pharaoh, but to the surrounding nations as well. Even more importantly, the Israelite people had not known me, nor my power, but these extreme actions certainly brought me to their attention.

I don't like describing it this way, but it's something you can relate to... it's like someone going on a blind date, but when they see who they are going out with, they are impressed. If the Israelites were going to be my people, they needed to be impressed with what I can do. And they had just seen me overcome the world's strongest nation, led by the world's strongest leader who was influenced by some of the world's greatest magicians.

Magic was not limited to the Old Testament; I showed it at least eight times in the writings of the New Testament. Why? Because just like Israel needed to see Me previously, the disciples and followers in the new era of the Church also needed to see that I was able to care and provide for them.

Within the confines of the New Testament, I compiled a number of occasions when 'magicians' confronted my disciples. This was done for several reasons:

- The magicians needed to be shown as inferior to Me;
- My disciples needed to be convinced there was no power greater than mine;
- The onlookers also needed proof of the God my followers were speaking about;
- The power sources (principalities, powers) needed to know they were inferior to me;

- This would be part of my "publicity campaign" to those wanting to know about Me;
- These power confrontations would show that Christianity cannot be tamed or retained by other powers, religions and magic;

Before heading into the New Testament power confrontations, let me restate our terminology.

Magic is an attempt to use supernatural beings for the benefit of the user or worshipper.

The use of it will lead to the belief and worship of other gods, rather than the one, true creator God of Christianity. To overcome the belief and loyalty of people to these false gods, Christianity will need to show itself victorious and overwhelmingly more powerful. Magic was to prevent people from seeing and worshipping the one true God... and that's why it must be overcome.

The Magic of Simon

The first magician my disciples recorded was with Simon (not to be mistaken for Simon Peter). Philip went down to the city of Samaria and began preaching to them and everyone seemed very interested in hearing my story, especially since the story was being backed up by miracles and signs. Many with unclean spirits were being freed from them and shouting as they went. That really drew some attention. Some who were paralyzed, and lame were also healed. So, there was a lot to be excited about. In that same area was a man named Simon who used to practice magic there. The people had been astounded and both he, and they, claimed him to be a great man. He was getting a lot of attention, and it was being said that he held great power from God (Acts 8:4-11).

Both, you and I, know his power was NOT from Me, but he disguised his real source of magic and allowed others to assume it was from God. The attention he was getting was not the problem, but his source of power for the magic would impede the going and growing of the gospel.

If the people saw two sources of power for life, they would be torn between the two and the magician was being lauded for being "divine." It was for that reason, Christianity must overcome both, the magic and the magician.

The magic Simon performed was something that would amaze people and exalt Simon. So something had to be done that would amaze people, but exalt Me. It came about that Simon was so awed by what he saw, he followed the disciples and was even baptized. But after that, he yearned for the power of the disciples so much that he offered to purchase it... and with that you begin to see the heart of Simon. He was still clamoring for the attention of the people and the power he once held. But Peter then spoke to him saying that he hoped Simon's silver would perish with him. You see, Peter saw through the smoke and mirrors and saw the lack of both, repentance and godliness that laid inside (Acts 8:18-24).

Peter called upon Simon to repent of his wickedness and told him he needed to seek forgiveness. Then Peter exposed Simon as having a gall of bitterness and being in bondage to unrighteousness.

I allowed this story to be included in your Bible to show the power of God vanquishing the power of magic. Now Adam, you should notice that this is no sleight-of-hand, no tricks or stagecraft. This was a demonic, evil power that was being called upon and my apostles had to take a stand against it.

The Magic of Elymas

There was also an occasion when my disciples came across a Jewish false prophet whose name was Bar-Jesus. I hope you noticed his name "bar-Jesus", which means he liked being called "my son" or "son of Jesus." He supposed that gave him a claim to credibility.

When the story begins, Elymas Bar-Jesus was already famous as a healer, but he was also known as a false prophet. His intention was to get close to the proconsul and turn him away from coming to faith in me.

As I've said previously, the purpose of magic and seeking its power is to turn followers from seeking me. This is the "calling card" of the magical and mystical arts… and that is the problem the apostle Saul (a.k.a. Paul) had with him.

Paul took a long gaze at Elymas and peered into his soul. You've read of occasions when I knew what was in the heart of people and on this occasion, so did Paul. Yes, Paul was filled with the Holy Spirit and fixed his gaze upon Elymas and what Paul saw was ugly to the core. Paul didn't mince his words either. He blatantly and boldly said the man was full of deceit and fraud. He called him a son of the devil (as opposed to being a son of Jesus) and an enemy to all righteousness.

You might not believe what happened next. Not only did Paul not pull his punches in words, neither did he in his actions either. He condemned the man to blindness so that he couldn't even see the sun for a while! If he was going to be blind in spirit – he may as well be blind in body too. With that, the so-called "son of Jesus" came to be seen as the "son of the devil."

This was another victory of the power of God over the world of magic. It nullified the power of magic and showed My supremacy.

The Magic of a Spirit of Divination

There was a third encounter with magic and Doctor Luke recorded the event this time. It began with my followers going to prayer and along the way they came across a servant-girl who had a spirit of divination. That is, a spirit resided within her and told her things others would not know (Acts 16).

Now, I want you to see that what she had to say was not false, but the source of her knowledge was from an entity that was not from Me. She cried out that these were men of the Most High God and that they were proclaiming the way of salvation. My disciples knew that what she was saying was true – but this was not a question of truth, it was a question of source. From where was she getting her information?

She persisted in pointing them out over several days, but finally, Paul was annoyed by it all. I don't need to remind you; Paul can deal with things decisively... and he did. Having had his fill of it, he commanded the spirit to leave her. And it did! Oh, her superiors were not happy with that – they had been making good money with her divination and all that came to a sudden stop.

I never said that the mystical and magical arts didn't work – I said that I forbid the use of them. Now before you ask, "Why forbid them if they are telling the truth?" Let me go ahead and answer that. The use of magical arts lent credibility to them, and credibility would draw followers away from me and the spread of the gospel. For the gospel to be seen and understood as the only true and supreme faith, it must be seen as superlative to them. If Paul had not dealt with her and the spirit within her, others would have been left believing her power was equal to God's and thereby, interrupt the spread of the gospel.

Divination had to be seen as evil (even though she was telling the truth) because it would lead to the belief and loyalty to the pagan gods instead of the true Creator God. They do not have your best interests at heart, but I do. One more time I need to say this so you never forget, all that is Good comes from Me. I am the source of it. Without me, there is no Good. And I want you to have it!

I love you so much that I will oppose anything that is second-rate. I will be the enemy of anything that isn't offering you the best. I come to give you *Life* and I want it to be *ABUNDANT!*

The Sons of Sceva

A fourth incident I want to point your eyes to was an exciting episode. This one did not involve my apostles, but it serves as a warning to any who want to become involved in spiritual warfare.

As you recall, a man named Sceva had sons that apparently wanted to be admired, so there came a day that some of them tried to cast out demons, but they were going to do this without my guidance or my authority.

Without my authority, they were defenseless. When they commanded the demons to come out, the response of the demon was something like, "I know Jesus... and I know about Paul... but who do you think you are to try to make me do anything?" And with that the demon jumped on them, beat them up and stripped them down. Those young men fled with wounds and without their clothes. Well, if they wanted attention – they certainly got it! And those who didn't see them streaking through the streets naked most assuredly heard about it (Acts 19:13-17).

The other result was that *fear fell upon both, Jews and Greeks who lived in the area and my name was greatly magnified.* And THAT is again the desired result of spiritual warfare.

Finally, let's talk about:

The Magic of Karma

Karma isn't actually "magic," but it is seen as a source of false belief. In short, Karma is the belief that "what goes around, comes around" and "you get what you deserve." It's a part of eastern thought and religion having to do with how you entered this life and how you leave this one for the next one.

This kind of thinking isn't restricted to eastern mysticism. This thinking is evident throughout many lands, cultures and time. Even back in the day of the apostle Paul's travels, there was an occasion that Paul, after a shipwreck, was picking up firewood and was bitten by a viper. It was ugly, because the viper wouldn't let go.

Paul stood there with this viper dangling from his hand and the onlookers began to say things like "undoubtedly, this man was a murderer and even though he didn't die in the sea, karma is going to get him, it is not going to let him live."

But you've read the story – you know what happened. Paul shook the creature off his hand and into the fire and he suffered no harm (Acts 28:1-5).

Setting minds right was not restricted to God showing his power over spirits and magicians. It also overcomes false ideas. False ideas like "karma" distract from the gospel and the power of Christ. These false ideas become strongholds in the life and minds of those who do not have me and that's why the gospel is powerful to the pulling down of strongholds.

I specifically directed Paul to teach about this. I told him that the weapons my followers will fight with are not of this world. But they are powerful, they have divine power and are able to pull down these false ideas, teachings and philosophies that detract from me.

This was a case in point. These men did not believe in magic, but they did believe in something that was not of God. Paul's actions were needed to bring the gospel and its power unimpeded to these men.

Adam, here's what I want you to take away from this: I am in the business of removing every obstacle that prevents the spread of my good news to mankind, whether it's a belief in magic, submitting one's self to false authorities or even a false belief, like Karma..

It is the good news of me that I am protecting. I want the good news of my "goodness" to spread. I want as many people as possible to hear about the Good I have for them and want to share with them.

Good enjoys spreading Good… and that's the gospel, that the Goodness of God has come and made a way for you to have it. Good news was vital for all men and nothing should be an obstacle to the gospel for men and women everywhere… and I do mean everywhere! My goal for the gospel is that it reaches people of every tongue, every tribe and every nation. That hasn't been accomplished yet, so the mission is still on—as The Battle Rages On…"

Removing every obstacle to people everywhere,

—Jesus

14

The Armor of God

Dear Jesus,

A lot of Christians talk about putting on the armor of God when dealing with spiritual warfare. It's difficult to go into a Christian bookstore without seeing the Bible verse Paul wrote about it being displayed on posters, wall-hangings, dish towels, t-shirts, hats, home decorations, keyrings, and more.

Even though spiritual warfare is talked about a lot, I don't really understand how one dresses with the items Paul talks about, and I don't see these battles taking place. Are we really expected to encounter spiritual battles and must we have all these elements covering us? And just how do you use them anyway.

Dressed in less,

—Adam

Dear Adam,

Even though you know the general idea of what Paul said, let's look at what Paul said:

> "Put on the whole armor of God, that you may be able to stand against the wiles of the devil. For we do not wrestle against flesh and blood, but against principalities, against powers, against the rulers of the darkness of this age, against spiritual hosts of wickedness in the heavenly places. Therefore, take up the whole armor of God, that you may be able to withstand in the evil day, and having done all, to stand.
>
> Stand therefore, having girded your waist with truth, having put on the breastplate of righteousness, and having shod your feet with the preparation of the gospel of peace; above all, taking the shield of faith with which you will be able to quench all the fiery darts of the wicked one. And take the helmet of salvation, and the sword of the Spirit, which is the word of God; praying always with all prayer and supplication in the Spirit, being watchful to this end with all perseverance and supplication for all the saints— and for me, that utterance may be given to me, that I may open my mouth boldly to make known the mystery of the gospel, for which I am an ambassador in chains; that in it I may speak boldly, as I ought to speak."
>
> *(Ephesians 6:10-19 NKJV)*

Yes, Paul summarized the need for being well-guarded and pro-tected during times of spiritual encounters. He remembered well what happened to those sons of Sceva and didn't want true followers grappling with the same circumstances.

However, I don't want you to use Paul's analogy to convince yourself that I've called you to spiritual wars. I have not. Yes, it's a great analogy, but you can take these few verses to mean something neither Paul, nor I, meant. I'll explain that as I go along, just bear with me.

Paul is understandably speaking to Christians, and he is en-couraging them to grow up in Christ and not be spiritual infants. Instead, they were to be mature, strong, aware and prepared.

Paul isn't leaving anything to chance. His warning to my follow-ers is that being successful in life for My Kingdom requires mature thinking, a thoroughness of thought, deeper roots in the Faith, and an awareness, steadfastness, and boldness in how they live in that Faith. Successful living and spreading of the Faith will necessitate an acknowledgement of spiritual things, a knowledge of how the spiritual realm works and not only a preparedness, but also being adequately equipped.

When I taught, I would sometimes refer to those who "have eyes to see and ears to hear" to let them see and hear the things of God. I can't emphasize it enough. Some things need to be spiritually discerned and that compels a devotion to understanding the things of God. Being 'smart' is not a pre-requisite, but being wise and discerning is crucial to observing and understanding the word, the will, and the ways of God.

When I chose my disciples, I didn't choose highly educated and powerful men. I didn't choose those who held high positions of authority in the world - and yet they ran circles around the religious scholars and rulers of their day. I have chosen the foolish things of the world to put to shame the wise. I have chosen the weak things of the world to put to shame the mighty.

I have chosen the base things of the world and the things that are despised so that no human could boast of what they have done. I did this so that when my followers accomplish great things, they know it was me working through them and they were not doing this alone (1 Cor 1:27-31).

This is what Paul meant by saying, "Be strong in the Lord." It meant to be firm, undoubting, assured, and confident, not only in what I said, but what I meant by the things I said. It means to be so assured that you cannot be swayed by something contradictory, or by any means that would deviate you from the exact meaning of what I did or meant. Adam, it's not enough to be confident of what my words were, but to know what they mean is essential.

You see, when Paul said, "Be strong in the Lord", he followed on with "and the strength of His might." He was making this distinction because it was all too easy for someone to depend on themselves. He understood that his greatest strength came when he felt the weakest and allowed me to work through him. When you are weak – that's when you will depend on me and you'll be amazed at what I can do through you.

In Paul's analogy of putting on armor, he used the phrase "the wiles of the devil." He was very apt in using that word "wiles." I've told you how the devil will disguise the contents of his "Box" and he'll giftwrap it so it looks so very, very appealing – but when you unwrap it, it is filled with deceit, trickery, guiles, ruses, subterfuge, scams, hoaxes… and ruin. I can't emphasize this enough – Satan is subtle, maneuvering, calculated, deceptive and crafty. Behind the attraction of his bait – there is a hook!

This is why it is imperative that you bring every thought into captivity and that you 'try' the spirits to see if they are from heaven or hell. Think about your thoughts and what you are asking. Clarify your words and your thoughts and weigh them with what you know of God and His ways. The wiles of the devil have had thousands of years to be perfected. He has crafted his research and resources and knows how to deceive (1 Corinthians 10:5; 1 John 4:1).

When Paul used that beautiful picture of putting on the armor, he did a great job in calling you to be prepared for what's ahead. But, as I said earlier – you should not mistake that as a "calling" to spiritual warfare. I told you I would explain that, so here's what I want you to know.

I called you to share the gospel with people. You were called to be "fishers of men." Yes, I know your songs are filled with courageous calls to be soldiers of the cross and to run head-long into spiritual battles, but that is not your Biblical calling.

And yes, along the way, you may encounter spiritual hosts and when that happens you are meant to withstand them. But your calling is to people… not battle. Don't mistake my words and meaning now, you are to be well-suited for wrestling with the principalities and powers and rulers of spiritual darkness AS YOU ENCOUNTER THEM, *but I never told you to seek them.* You are to seek people.

While seeking people, I will expect you to stand firm in the opposition to spiritual forces, but only when it happens as you fulfill your primary target… People!

Look back at my life on earth. You don't see me seeking devils and demons. I encountered them while serving people. I sent the apostles out in pairs to seek people and share the gospel. While tending to that, if they encountered spiritual opposition, they would deal with that. But notice, they weren't sent out to deal with spiritual opposition, they were sent to minister to people.

So, let me restate the priorities:

Do—Seek people and deal with demons

Do Not—Seek demons and deal with people

That's the way I did it. I came to serve and seek that which was lost and I dealt with spiritual forces along the way. But my primary purpose in coming was not to deal with the spiritual opposition. Oh yes, it did happen, but I focused on the people.

Unfortunately, Paul's admonition sometimes sounds like the clarion call to arms and too many focus on that rather than on the people I sent them to serve. Understand this – Paul was using an allegory… a simile… a picture of yourselves as warriors. And maybe you need that to spur you on and keep you encouraged. But don't forget, it's just an allegory… a mental picture.

You should be resolute, steadfast, mature, strong and withstand the wiles of the devil, but your calling is to people.

Take a moment, quit looking at the analogy itself – that is, don't focus on the pieces of armor, but instead lay your attention on what each piece represents. Paul mentioned several items in his checklist:

- Truth
- Righteousness
- Gospel of peace
- Faith
- Salvation
- Spirit
- Prayer
- Supplication

- Watching

- Perseverance

THIS is the powerhouse that equips you to deal with ministering in the strength of Me. These are the words that should be imprinted on the coffee mugs, keychains, t-shirts and other merchandise in the Christian bookstores! These are the marks of those who are growing deep. These are the attributes of those who are maturing, know the Word and who consider the whole counsel of God.

Let me now draw your attention to one very small, but very important detail:

Are your feet to be shod with the gospel of peace?

No.

Read it again.

Your feet are *not* to be shod with the gospel of peace, but with the *preparation of* the gospel of peace.

What Paul was trying to convey to you was, "BE READY" to go. There's no time for someone to say, "Let me put my shoes on first." You were being implored to be always ready to share the peace that only God can give. Not only ready to share the gospel, but ready to give a proper reason for the faith that is in you.

I used different words, but with the same meaning, when I had Paul write to Timothy, imploring him to be ready in season and out of season to reprove, rebuke, and exhort with complete patience and teaching.

Be ready, Adam. Be ready to share the gospel and maintain a spirit of peace about you always. Be ready to give reasons for your faith. Be ready when I return. Live on the edge of your seat… READY for whatever, whenever!

Unless there is an obvious demoniac confronting you, how will you know when you are encountering spiritual warfare? Satan's main device is not to confront you with malevolent and formidable evil... no, not at all. Rather, he has honed his craft and in his wily charm, he will sneak into your mind.

Yes, the mind is the primary battlefield.

It's not the obvious obstructions to my cause that will disarm you, it's the chicanery of tip toeing into your thoughts and mind. This is where he will cause you to question the will and the ways of God. He did it effectively with Eve...

- He probed God's words... "Did God say...?"
- He alluded to the idea that God might be lying... "You will not die."
- And he questioned God's motives... "For God knows...." (Genesis 3:1-6)
- He then tried the same with Me: (Matthew 4:1-11)
- He questioned my identity... "If you are the Son of God, command these stones..."
- He challenged God's ways... "If you are the Son of God, throw yourself down..."
- He probed my allegiance and loyalty... "If you will fall down and worship me..."

At the risk of being repetitive – it bears repeating. I remind you of Paul's petitioning to all believers, take every thought into captivity and to try the spirits to see if they are of Me (2 Corinthians 10:5 and 1 John 4:1).

Why does Satan use these tactics? The answer is obvious – it's because they work! He uses them so well after thousands of years of practice. All the while, by working in your mind, you don't even think he is present – you are under the impression these are your thoughts!

This is why I confronted Simon Peter with a warning. I told him that Satan has demanded to have him, that he might sift Peter like wheat... but I also comforted him, assuring him that I would pray for him (Luke 22:31).

This is why you need to think in terms of being outfitted with the armor of God. But, again, I implore you to not get caught up in the flowery analogy of armor, but to find your sustenance in what the armor represents, that's what's important.

By now you are familiar with my "Jesus Box" and Satan's "Other Box". Now it's time to make "Your Box" Take unto, into and onto yourself:

Your Box

Truth	Righteousnes	Gospel of peace
Faith	Salvation	Spirit,
Prayer	Supplication	Watching
Perseverance		

These are the ingredients and characteristics that are to be emphasized more than the analogy of body armor.

Look back at those comforting words I spoke to Peter... "but I have prayed for you." Adam, how do you think that would make you feel if I said those same words to you? Would it be an emboldening concept – to know that I was praying for you? Even though you live two thousand years after I said those words to Peter – they can, and do, apply to you. That's one of the responsibilities of the Holy Spirit. In the same way, the Spirit will help you in your weakness.

When you don't know what to do, and when you don't know how to pray, the Spirit will intercede for you. He will search your heart and use words you don't even comprehend to get your needs before the Father (Romans 8:26-27).

This is what I meant when I told my disciples that I needed to go away. They resisted that idea, but it was for their own betterment. If I went back to the Father, I would not leave them without some comfort – I would leave them in the hands of the Holy Spirit, who would intercede for them in ways they could not even fathom.

When a child is scared and their father offers them his presence and his hand, it's a genuine source of comfort and a great reason to be emboldened. *That* is what I offer through the Holy Spirit and for that reason – if you are appropriately outfitted, you can not only withstand the wiles of the devil, but you will be bold to pull down the strongholds of thought Satan has built in the minds and hearts of our opponents.

You will not only be able to convince them or overcome them, but you will be rightly prepared to "take on the world". And that's the goal I have set before you... Go into all the world, convincing them and overcoming the gates of hell that prevent them from knowing Me.

With that attitude, you will have the right mind and right pri-orities so that as you seek people you will be right-minded to contend with devils.

Now that you know this – you'll better understand how "the battle rages on..."

Adam, go get'em!

—Jesus

15

Collision in Colossians

Dear Jesus,

I'm learning so much, but in doing so I'm discovering how I've failed you so many times. I haven't been bold in sharing the faith and, to be honest, I've struggled and fallen so far short of what you want for me.

I'm sorry.

I feel like I'm one of your greatest disappointments. I thought of myself as a grand warrior decked out in Holy Spirit armor, but I've failed you. What do I do now?

Disappointingly yours,

—Adam

Dear Adam,

Ha! Now, don't get me wrong, I'm not laughing at you, but while we're having all these discussions where you long to grow and mature, let me assure you that you are *far* from my greatest disappointment.

The New Testament points to others who missed the mark far worse than you. And the book is there to show them how to get back on track. The entirety of the book of Colossians was a letter to the church at Colossae and it was a cry to that particular church to turn around. Just like you and so many others, they missed the mark too! You see, after being won to Me, the whole church was being tricked into following false gods and the worship of angels.

Yes, I can imagine the surprise on your face to learn that but read it more carefully now and you'll see this is what was happening. After great doctrinal teaching about me won their hearts and minds, they were on a collision course going against all they had been taught.

I'll bet you were taught that the book was primarily about my preeminence. And, it's true, that is what the first part of the book is about. But now ask *why* did they need to be taught this? If they had received tremendous doctrinal teaching, why did they need this reminder? It was because they came off the rails and their faith was de-railing fast.

The church was being tricked into worshiping lesser gods and fallen angels and that is why Paul put so much emphasis on my preeminence. He had to remind them that I was far above all angels to bring their thinking, their devotion and their hearts back to Me before they slipped too far away to recover. For this reason, Paul speaks to them about things in heaven, elemental spiritual forces and more. Paul was determined that they understood that, in Me and through Me, all things were created. And that meant ALL things.

It included all things in both, heaven and earth… those things that were visible and those that were invisible (Colossians 1:16).

I will assume that when you read this previously, you were caught up in the idea of My excellency. And, of course, that is what Paul was pointing to. But when that's all you see and read there, you miss the other revelation, so don't skip over that portion. Here, let me remind you of what he wrote:

> "For in Him, all things were created: things in heaven
> and on earth, visible and invisible; whether thrones,
> or powers, or rulers or authorities;
>
> *(Colossians 1:16; NIV)*

By not dismissing the last part of that sentence you'll see that what Paul was emphasizing was my preeminence over the lesser powers (thrones, powers, rulers, authorities). He was admonishing the Colossians to think about what they were doing. He's asking why give homage to the demonic powers and lesser powers when there is one who is not only of higher authority, but He is the very creator of those they were being tempted to worship?

Paul then went on to bring the Father into the discussion. He said, God, the Father, was pleased that in Me, would dwell all the fullness of Himself and that all things would be reconciled to Him through Me, and that included things on both, earth and heaven (Colossians 1:19).

That was followed by Paul's entreaty for the church to stay with, or continue worshiping, me, rather than those that were less than me. In essence, he was saying that they had been established in my gospel, and they should stay with it.

He was encouraging them to continue in their faith, to be established and firm, and not to move from the hope that was held out in the gospel preached to them. This is the same gospel that they had heard, and it was the gospel that was being proclaimed to every creature under heaven (Colossians 1:23).

When you search your Bible, you'll notice that you have each book broken down into chapters and verses. I want you to realize that wasn't the way it was written. After all, you don't write your mother an email broken down into verses and chapters. Understanding that, you'll realize that Paul didn't "start another chapter" – he just kept writing and kept putting the pressure on the Church to continue in me and to resist being drawn away.

He reminded them that all the treasures of wisdom and knowledge were to be found in me. He did this so they would not be deceived by fine-sounding arguments. Do you see how this fits back into what I was telling you in my last letter? – The deceitfulness and the devilry of Satan is found in your mind. Satan will put up great sounding arguments, but they are false, and he does it to steal you away from me. What more could the church want than to find the "treasures of wisdom and knowledge" in me?

After this, Paul doubled back to pick up any strays who still had doubts. Once again, his pleading goes to the heart of his message:

> "So then, just as you received Christ Jesus as Lord,
> continue to live your lives in him, rooted and built up
> in him, strengthened in the faith as you were taught."
> *(Colossians 2:6; NIV)*

And you know how Paul could be a bulldog when it came to doctrinal teaching. He didn't let up on his argument, nor his reasoning in calling them to true spiritual worship, rather than something designed or reasoned by men. He pounded his teaching home by saying:

> "See to it that *no one takes you captive* through hollow and deceptive philosophy, which depends on human tradition and the elemental *spiritual forces of this world.*"
>
> *(Colossians 2:8; NIV).*

Then, Paul, being a great debater, proceeds with his argument that I am ultimate… and there is nothing to be had or gained without Me, for I am the head of it all (Colossians 2:9).

Apparently, those who would persuade the church otherwise, had made up high-sounding arguments and encouraged the church to observe dietary restrictions and festivals for those (gods and angels) they would worship. So, Paul took that into consideration in his arguments.

> "Therefore, do not let anyone judge you by what you eat or drink, or with regard to a religious festival, a new moon celebration or a Sabbath day. These are a shadow of the things that were to come; the reality, however, is found in Christ."
>
> *(Col 2:16-17 NIV)*

Notice that in the next verse, Paul argues there is a reference to how those others hold themselves. He said that these ideas come not from a spiritual source, but an *un*spiritual mind and can result in being turned away from Christ. He said,

> "Don't let anyone who delights in false humility and the worship of angels, disqualify you. Such a person also goes into great detail about what they have seen; they are puffed up with idle notions *by their unspiritual mind.*"
>
> *(Col 2:16-17 NIV)*

Some of the false leaders started with me, but then fell into false worship. They disqualified themselves from me, as well as those they take with them, in their thinking. They have lost their way and have become disconnected from both me and the church (Colossians 2:19).

Paul's arguments end with reasonable thoughts about those who think there might be something more apart from Me. He said,

> "Since you died with Christ to the elemental spiritual forces of this world, why, as though you still belonged to the world, do you submit to its rules: "Do not handle! Do not taste! Do not touch!"? These rules, which have to do with things that are all destined to perish with use, are based on merely human commands and teachings."
>
> *(Colossians 2:20-23 NIV)*

Adam, the church was not left "wondering" about what to do. If they are not to follow these false teachers, if there is nothing more, how then should they live and worship? Paul didn't leave anything to chance. That man was thorough in his thinking, his teaching and his arguments. I knew he was the man for the job when I encountered him on his way to Damascus. He said it this way:

> "Since then, you have been raised with Christ, set your hearts on things above, where Christ is, seated at the right hand of God. Set your minds on things above, not on earthly things. For you died, and your life is now hidden with Christ in God. When Christ, who is your life, appears, then you also will appear with him in glory."
>
> *(Colossians 3:1-4 NIV)*

If they want more they will get it, if they stay in me. For if they follow me, they will appear with me in GLORY! How could anyone want more than that?

The book of Colossians is about the preeminence of Christ, but why? It was because believers were being pulled away from right thinking and full understanding of what they had heard about me.

Adam, this is how spiritual warfare works. It's subtle - it's not like the days when giants were confronted. There are no blazing lights or blaring horns, no vast armies of the enemy that you see, it can happen quietly, surreptitiously.

Does that sound any different from what you see and hear in churches in your day? No. Why? – Because Satan is crafty, deft, devious, clever and skilled in how he influences people – even my followers. What he was doing back then, he is still doing today. His purpose, his tactics and his goals have not changed.

And that's why I keep insisting The Battle Rages On..."

Preeminently yours,

—Jesus

CHAPTER

16

The Battles to Come

Dear Jesus,

If the church in Colossae, having started so strong, could go so wrong, what does that say about the rest of us? Thank you for showing me that things are happening that I can't see.

I admit that it all makes me wonder what the future will be for mankind. What's left while we wait for your second appearance? How bad can it get here? What roles will heaven and earth have to play before the end?

Fearfully yours,

—*Adam*

Dear Adam,

Yes, thinking about what lies ahead can raise some fear. There are battles yet to be fought. Even though there has been a transfer of authority from the principalities and powers over the nations, that doesn't mean they've laid down their weapons or attitudes.

I wish more people understood that those powers will not quit, nor give up until they are overcome. Their goal is not just to deceive humanity – it is to bring ruination upon you and to destroy you. It's because you are so near and dear to me and the Father and they want to hurt us and you, and destroy our plans and our hopes for all humanity.

You were made in my image. You are image-bearers of me. You are so important to my heart that I willingly left Glory and came here to die, just because I want to share all that is *good* with you and through you!

Humanity is not some prize to win for them – instead, humanity is something to destroy and tear away from me. Whether it's to despise me, or to ruin what I cherish, their goal is not to bring benevolence to you. Remember, they are here to steal, to kill, and to destroy.

Even though I had all authority delivered to me, there are still major spiritual wars yet to come. They will be the worst that earth and mankind have ever endured. Yes, there have been skirmishes and battles before, but major upheavals are in the future.

Before venturing into what's ahead, I want to take you on a remedial course of what spiritual warfare has looked like in the past. While there are many, many episodes I could point you to, allow me to start with an event that resulted in a war of "biblical proportions."

Assyria had a vast army that was threatening my people. So, that very night I killed 185,000 soldiers of the King of Assyria (2

Kings 19; 32-36). Notice now, it wasn't a legion of angels, it wasn't the army of the hosts of heaven, it wasn't a multitude of heavenly soldiers - that was just me in my form as the Angel of the Lord. I am very capable of handling spiritual battles.

(Note from author: For more on this, see my book, "Before I Was Jesus" on Amazon or Barnes and Noble books).

But let's keep going and look at an event you are much more familiar with – how about the time David was going to fight the giant, Goliath? David turned what was purely an earthly battle into one that was fraught with spiritual implications. He was willing to do battle with a man of gigantic proportions because he said Goliath had defied the armies of the living God. He declared to King Saul that since I had delivered him out of both, the paw of a lion and a bear, that I would also deliver him out of the hand of the Philistine.

And David's faith didn't stop with memories. Oh, no. He looked the giant in the eyes and prophesied that "This day the Lord will deliver you into my hand, and I will smite you and cut off your head. I will give the corpses of the army to the birds of the air and the wild beasts of the earth, SO THAT ALL THE EARTH MAY KNOW THERE IS A GOD IN ISRAEL" David was now making what appeared to be an earthly warzone into a spiritual battlefield (1 Samuel 17:1-47).

Then, let's recall the story of Daniel and the lions den. Daniel's king had been influenced into signing an edict that anyone who prayed to anyone other than the king would be thrown to the lions. Daniel was found praying to me and he was indeed to be a morsel of meat for the lions. However, Daniel's impeccable spiritual life had made an impact on the king. The king himself knew he had been manipulated and pleaded that Daniel's God, whom Daniel served continually, would deliver him.

Daniel knew the spiritual realm had been involved through his night among the big cats. The next day, he was found alive and said that I sent an angel to preserve him. (Daniel 6). And, Adam, did you notice how that story ended? – The king wrote to all the peoples, nations and languages in the known earth saying that people should fear the God of Daniel.

I want you to make a note of this, Adam, these battles were not just about the person or the "hero" in the story. This may come as a shock to you, but you may as well learn it now. Neither creation, nor these battles, were just about you and humanity. It has never been just about getting you forgiven, saved and into heaven. All creation was by Me, through Me, and for Me. And it's the same way with these battles.

Yes, my death on the cross was for the atoning you needed, but don't forget my ultimate plan has always been about propagating my goodness and sharing it throughout all my creation. Good loves to produce more good! Of course, making a way for you and others to enter heaven has been a part of that plan, but the plan is bigger than that!

Let's not forget about the spiritual beings I created before I created humanity. Some chose to be loyal servants while others did not. They sinned and then brought more sin into the very nature of all mankind. And, if that wasn't enough, Satan and his angels have fought against my purposes, even to the extent that all creation has been groaning under the effect of sin (Romans 8:19-23).

I could continue with Shadrach, Meshach, and Abednego... I could go on about those I rescued from devils in my earthly life. These events of the past I'm bringing back to your mind for a purpose.

Adam, who won the battles? Me!

Who made David a victor? Me!

Who protected Daniel and extinguished his foes? Me!

Who walked in the fire with Shadrach, Meshach, and Abed-nego? Me!

Who cast out the demons, confronted the devils and withstood the temptations of Satan? Me!

Who really won at Calvary, in spite of being crucified? Me!

This is why Paul was so concerned about the church in Colossae. They had forgotten Me! That I was the victor! Always have been, and always will be. That is why Paul was preaching of my preeminence!

Here's the lesson from the past before we look at the future – "I Win!" I did then. I do now. I will in the days ahead. So, while I could just go on and on about the battles of the past, let's look ahead, while already knowing: I Win.

There are three great battlefields left and they have been spoken and written about since the days of the Old Testament prophets. They include:

- The Tribulation (3-1/2 years);
- The Great Tribulation (3-1/2 years);
- Armageddon

And they involve:

- Satan
- The False Prophet
- The Anti-Christ
- The minions, beasts and demons allegiant to Satan

Since the days of the Old Testament, there has been much prophecy about the days of tribulation to come. According to the prophets, there will be 3-1/2 years of tribulation followed by another 3-1/2 years of "great" tribulation, then the battle of Armageddon followed by 1,000 years of peace and finally, one even greater battle where Satan and all his minions are finally and forever defeated.

These are pivotal points in the history of mankind. Prophecies have been made, the course has been determined and nothing will prevent it from happening as it has been foretold.

The two 3-1/2 year periods make up a seven-year span that goes by the moniker "The Tribulation." The first half is a tribulation period, but the second half is much worse.

There are indicators given when it is on the horizon. Scriptures describe it this way:

- An abundance of false teachers within the Church.
- False ideas and delusions about false religions.
- Greater martyrdom of Christians.
- An abandonment from Christianity and righteousness.
- Abundant wars and rumors of wars.
- World-wide catastrophes.
- Food supply interruptions… and much, much more.

Eschatological beliefs are centered around these events. There are those who believe the Church will be raptured out of the world before, mid-way and after the tribulation.

These are known as the *Pre-*Trib, *Mid-*Trib and *Post-*Tribulation positions.

The faithful Christians will be tried, tired and tormented.

Adam, you've noticed many of the signs and wonders I've done were to point observers to God. But did you notice that sometimes to do the supernatural, I take the natural and just add my "super?" For instance, I took the Red Sea, which was quite natural… and the wind which was quite natural, but then the waters blew back and parted leaving dry ground SUPER-naturally for Moses and Israel to walk through.

In a similar way, I took the water of the Sea of Galilee, which was natural… and the wind from the mountains, which was natural… and used the storm (natural) for me to walk on water, which was very SUPER-natural.

I took a man, blind from birth, which is unfortunate, but natural… and I took clay, which is natural… and then I healed the man's eyes, which was, again, very SUPER-natural.

I say this to add this thinking to the signs of the last days and the natural disasters that will be demonstrated during that time. The ocean will turn to blood, there will be earthquakes and darkness, mountains will move, stars will seemingly fall from the sky and water will become poisoned.

Those on earth who see these things will be overwhelmed or they may make up natural explanations as to why these things are happening. But the Bible's description of those days depicts a time so awful that people will seek to die.

While it is a terrible thing to fall into the hands of an angry God, it will also be awful to live during a time when demons from hell run rampant throughout the earth.

Reading from just a few small portions of the book of Revelation, you'll begin to see the devastation caused by demonic forces during this time:

"And there went out another horse that was red: and power was given to him that sat thereon to take peace from the earth, and that they should kill one another: and there was given unto him a great sword."

—Revelations 6:4 (KJV)

"And I looked and beheld a pale horse: and his name that sat upon him was Death, and Hell followed with him. And power was given unto them over the fourth part of the earth, to kill with the sword, and with hunger and with death and with the beasts of the earth."

—Revelations 6:8 (KJV)

"There was a great earthquake; and the sun became black as sackcloth of hair and the moon became as blood; and the stars of heaven fell unto the earth even as a fig tree casts her untimely figs, when she is shaken of a mighty wind. And the heaven departed as a scroll when it is rolled together; and every mountain and island were moved out of their places. And the kings of the earth, and the great men, and the rich men, and the chief captains, and the mighty men, and every bondman and every free man hid themselves in the dens and in the rocks of the mountains."

—Revelations 6:12-15 (KJV)

The third part of the trees was burnt up and all green grass was burnt up... a great mountain burning with fire was cast into the sea: and the third part of the sea became blood and the third part of the creatures which were in the sea and had life, died, and the third part of the ships were destroyed.

—Revelations 8:7-9 (KJV)

And remember, what you just read is only a small portion of what the book tells us. And, as bad as it is... it's not over.

"I saw a star fall from heaven unto the earth: and to him was given the key of the bottomless pit. And he opened the bottomless pit; and there arose a smoke out of the pit, as the smoke of a great furnace; and the sun and the air were darkened by reason of the smoke of the pit. And there came out of the smoke locusts upon the earth and unto them was given power as the scorpions of the earth have power."

—Revelations 9:1-3 (KJV)

"So the four angels, who had been prepared for the hour, the day, the month, and the year, were released to kill a third of mankind. The number of mounted troops was twice ten thousand times ten thousand; I heard their number. And this is how I saw the horses in my vision and those who rode them: they wore breastplates the color of fire and of sapphire and of sulfur, and the heads of the horses were like lions' heads, and fire and smoke and sulfur came out of their mouths. By these three plagues a third of mankind was killed, by the fire and smoke and sulfur coming out of their mouths. For the power of the horses is in their mouths and in their tails, for their tails are like serpents with heads, and by means of them they wound."

—Revelations 9:15-19 (KJV)

"And I saw a beast rising out of the sea, with ten horns and seven heads, with ten diadems on its horns and blasphemous names on its heads. And the beast that I saw was like a leopard; its feet were like a bear's, and its mouth was like a lion's mouth. And to it the dragon gave his power and his throne and great authority. One of its heads seemed to have a mortal wound, but its mortal wound was healed, and the whole earth marveled as they followed the beast. And they worshiped the dragon, for he had given his authority to the beast, and they worshiped the beast, saying, "Who is like the beast, and who can fight against it?"

—*Revelations 13:1-4 (KJV)*

The dread of the days to come should fill your heart. This will be a time of absolute terror and devastation. And it's all part of the spiritual wars to come.

However, I will be able to overcome... and I will. Only those who have given themselves to me will spend eternity with me. One of the last things I told my disciples was that it was necessary for me to go away (by ascending into heaven) so I could prepare a place for us together.

"Now I saw heaven opened, and behold, a white horse. And He who sat on him was called Faithful and True, and in righteousness He judges and makes war. His eyes were like a flame of fire, and on His head were many crowns. He had a name written that no one knew except Himself. He was clothed with a robe dipped in blood, and His name is called The Word of God. And the armies in heaven, clothed in fine linen, white and clean, followed Him on white horses. Now out of His mouth goes a sharp sword, that with it He should strike the nations. And He Himself will rule them with a rod of iron. He Himself treads the winepress of the fierceness and wrath of Almighty God. And He has on His robe and on His thigh a name written: KING OF KINGS AND LORD OF LORDS."

—Revelations 19:11-16 (NKJV)

And the work is carried on by angels at my beckoning:

"Then I saw an angel coming down from heaven, having the key to the bottomless pit and a great chain in his hand. He laid hold of the dragon, that serpent of old, who is the Devil and Satan, and bound him for a thousand years; and he cast him into the bottomless pit, and shut him up, and set a seal on him, so that he should deceive the nations no more till the thousand years were finished. But after these things he must be released for a little while. And I saw thrones, and they sat on them, and judgment was committed to them. Then I saw the souls of those who had been beheaded for their witness to Jesus and for the word of God, who had not worshiped the beast or his image, and had not received his mark on their foreheads or on their hands. And they lived and reigned with Christ for a thousand years. But the rest of the dead did not live again until the thousand years were finished. This is the first resurrection. Blessed and holy is he who has part in the first resurrection. Over such the second death has no power, but they shall be priests of God and of Christ, and shall reign with Him a thousand years. Now when the thousand years have expired, Satan will be released from his prison and will go out to deceive the nations which are in the four corners of the earth, Gog and Magog, to gather them together to battle, whose number is as the sand of the sea. They went up on the breadth of the earth and surrounded the camp of the saints and the beloved city. And fire came down from God out of heaven and devoured them. The devil, who deceived them, was cast into the lake of fire and brimstone where the beast and the false prophet are. And they will be tormented day and night forever and ever."

—Revelations 20:1-10 (NKJV)

And so it is... as you can plainly see, from this day until then... *"The Battle Rages On..."*

Stay brave and firm, Adam

—Jesus

17

It is, and Isn't, Finished

Dear Jesus,

When I read about the last days of your earthly life, I was shaken when coming to the scene of your crucifixion. It was horrible and it had to be excruciatingly painful. I want to say, "It shouldn't have happened," but I see that it was the means of you paying for our sins. It was the process of our salvation. Thank you so much for that!

But just before you commended your spirit into the hands of your Father, you said those words that are etched into the memories of all who have heard the story, "It is finished."

There's been a lot of speculation about the meaning of that statement. Were you referring to the end of your earthly life and ministry? Were you referring to something we were not aware of? I'm a bit perplexed about this.

Still wanting to learn,

—*Adam*

Dear Adam,

Even after all we've discussed, you are as curious as ever. I admire that, so keep it up!

So, you are wanting to know WHAT was finished with my statement on the cross. Well, there were many things that needed to be completed for my time on earth to have been totally successful. Until all were fulfilled, it was NOT finished. So, let's talk about those.

- *First*, my earthly life had to fulfill a host of prophecies including where and when I was born, my genealogy and more. That was fulfilled.

- *Secondly*, I had to live a sinless life. That was done.

- *Thirdly*, there were certain miracles and signs I needed to do to verify my claim as the Messiah. That was completed.

- *Fourthly*, I selected my disciples and poured myself into them, leaving them as the team that would continue My messages and begin the work of taking the gospel to the Gentiles, as well as the Jews. That was done too.

- *Fifthly... and finally*, my very death, the method of it and the timing of it had to fulfill all the many prophecies uttered over many, many years.

Mere days before my soon-coming death, I entered the eastern gate of Jerusalem with crowds of people shouting "Hosanna," while making a path for me with their cloaks. I rode into the city on a donkey that had not been ridden before. The gate I entered was the same gate... and on the same day, the High Priest would make his way from Bethlehem with the approved sacrificial lamb for the Passover and the Day of Atonement. They just didn't know that I was going to be the *real* sacrificial lamb... nor did they know that was the plan my Father and I devised before the world was even created.

Remember Adam, none of this caught us by surprise! Not even the part yet to come. You see, there was more prophecy that needed to be fulfilled.

I was to be beaten, stripped and striped by a whip, jeered and spat upon. And finally, I was crucified, but with no bones broken. Even while on the cross, I was given vinegar instead of water, just as the Psalms prophesied. And I was to die at the same time and on the same day that the Passover lamb was being killed.

Yes, while I would rise from the dead three days later and minister to my followers, all the requirements of my earthly ministry were now finished. It was true, "It is finished." With my sinless life and atoning death, I satisfied all claims. I poured myself out as a propitiation and calmed the anger of God the Father against sin. For thirty-three years, I was limited by the confines of a human body. I was tempted, tired and worn. The price for sin had been paid and all of that was now finished.

However, that didn't mean everything was finished… just the part my earthly body played. There were still things, important things, yet to be done. Some of that was accomplished while my body laid in the grave. And even more would be done after my resurrection.

For me, there was not only life after death – there was *work* after death too. Just because my earthly body was dead doesn't mean "I" was dead. No, there was still much needing to be done.

So, the story of my earthly ministry was finished, but several things would have been left undone if my story stopped there. The principalities and powers had to be dealt with, death had to be overcome, a resurrection accomplished, and I still had my ascension back into heaven to look forward to.

While still in my earthly body, I dealt directly and authoritatively with the principalities and powers, but how I dealt with them while my body was in the tomb would surprise even them. What I did during those three days and three nights still mystifies many, so let me clear it up for you.

I'm sure you recall our earlier discussion about the angels who married human women and created Nephilim, or giants. I mentioned that they were arrested and imprisoned where they remain while awaiting judgment. These were angels who left their first estate and domain as part of a plot to deflect my coming (2 Peter 2 and Jude 6).

Now that I was not limited to my earthly body, it was now time to confront them. But the conflict was not limited to just them. I was about to make an open show to them and those onlooking spirits, demons, and spiritual rulers. Yes, all those who rebelled, fell and worked against the Father's plan, were about to see what they had done and how the tables were turned against them.

These spirits had an overall strategy to disregard the Father's plan, step out from the umbrella of my reign and authority, bring humanity to their own destruction and set up their own world and governance. They attempted to thwart my coming. When that didn't work, they endeavored to deceive me, trick me, beat me and kill me.

Most readers will recognize that all previous attempts to destroy me failed. I escaped Bethlehem's killing of the babies, I walked through the crowd that wanted to throw me off a cliff, and it just wasn't my time to die when they wanted to stone me... and when I did finally die, they thought the battle was over.

But had they known what would happen next, they never would have killed me (1 Corinthians 2:7-8).

Again, not being restrained by my human body, I decided to confront them all and show them how they played into the hands of my Father and me. Yes, I went directly to them. Just as the Spirit one time led me to Satan to be tempted, this time, He led me to the spirits in prison, and I proclaimed my victory over them as well as my new authority. The Father was now giving me the authority over the gentile nations that many of these spirits once controlled.

Peter mentioned this when he said that it was by the Spirit that I went and preached to the spirits in prison (1 Peter 3:18). He wasn't recording that I preached to the humans who died and were in hell. No. And he wasn't referring to the dead who were in Paradise. And, when he used the word "preached" – he was not referencing what you might hear on any Sunday morning.

The word Peter was using meant to "proclaim," You might say I was boasting a bit and retaking the authority over the gentile nations. When you finish reading what Peter had to say, it's quite clear that I was proclaiming victory over the fallen angels. He didn't leave any other options when he said I…

> "proclaimed to the spirits in prison, because they formerly did not obey, when God's patience waited in the days of Noah,"
>
> *—1 Peter 3:19-20*

Let's see what else Peter had to say and then we'll look at Jude's writing too.

> "For if God did not spare angels when they sinned, but cast them into hell and committed them to chains of gloomy darkness to be kept until the judgment;"
>
> *—2 Peter 2:4 (ESV)*

> "And the angels who did not stay within their own position of authority, but left their proper dwelling, he has kept in eternal chains under gloomy darkness until the judgment of the great day."

—*Jude 6*

My proclamation of victory before these angels was a provoking confrontation showing that all their many plans were for nothing. Despite their many attempts to prevent my arrival on planet earth or from achieving mankind's salvation, there I stood.

But that wasn't the only victory announcement I was making. I also disarmed the principalities and powers that were not imprisoned. I disarmed the rulers and authorities and put them to open shame, by triumphing over them (Colossians 2:15).

Paul used an unusual phrase when mentioning this elsewhere. He spoke of me leading "captivity captive." Unfortunately, that's not a common phrase in your day so it leaves you perplexed and wondering, "What does that mean?"

When Paul wrote that, it was a reference to Roman conquerors returning from battle and bringing the live enemies in chains. There would be a lot of pomp and circumstance, a lot of celebration, when a conqueror would return with the enemies in chains and bondage. The celebration was to put on display those enemies who wanted to subjugate them, being put in subjugation themselves. Those who had threatened them with captivity were now captives themselves. After a bit of celebration, the living enemies were then put to death and gifts were distributed to the people from the spoils of war.

With that analogy, I not only conquered my enemies, but made an open shame of them. I put them on display as those who once held power and authority, but who are now themselves ridiculed and made to be a spectacle.

How sweet it was. Paul also referred to this in his letter to the church at Ephesus when he quoted Hosea 13:14:

"O death, where is your victory?

O death, where is your sting?"

"The sting of death is sin, and the power of sin is the
law. But thanks be to God, who gives us the victory
through our Lord Jesus Christ."
—*1 Corinthians 15:55 (ESV)*

Now, Adam, as good as that moment was, there was still more to
accomplish before my work was complete.

Here's another Bible word that may need some explanation:
"propitiation." This was one of my very important jobs, so don't
skip over it just because the word is unfamiliar to you. I was your
"propitiation."

Allow me a moment to draw a word picture for you. Suppose a
husband and wife had a big argument, it descends into heated anger
and insults are thrown. Let's suppose he leaves the house and goes
to a friend. He sulks, complains, but finally he decides to go home.
Perhaps enough time has passed that he and his wife can just forget
about the argument and move on.

But, when he described the argument to his friend, he relayed
the last insult he left his wife with… and it was a crippling comment.
It was one that would be felt for a very long time. So, his friend
suggests that the husband stop at a store and buy some flowers,
maybe some chocolate and even a new dress for his wife. And so
he does. But the friend also suggested that the man not just barge
into the house, rather, he should stop, ring the doorbell, maybe even
get on his knees and hold the gifts as a token to his wife when he
approaches the door.

So, picture him now as he gathers the items, rings the bell, drops
to one knee and when his wife approaches the door, he immediately
holds up these gifts before ever saying a word.

Now picture her just before he arrives. She's filled to the brim with anger, hurt and more. But, when she opens the door, she is pacified by the tokens of remorse, and her anger is calmed enough to hear her husband's apology. The token calmed her anger so she could listen. His apologies were heard, and she gave her forgiveness... and, of course, they lived happily ever after.

Now that you have the picture in your mind – let me explain. The gifts that calmed her anger, well, those were the PROPITIA-TION. It was my willing and voluntary death that calmed the anger of God against your sins and made it possible for your repentance to be heard before God.

Adam, let me emphasize it once again - I was *YOUR* propiti-ation.

Before you think we're finished... we're not. Even after all this, there was still more that had to be undertaken. With my resurrection, there was to be a "Transfer of Authority." That which was once held captive was to be under new management.

This is why I waited until after the resurrection to say,

> "All authority in heaven and on earth has been given
> to me. Go therefore and make disciples of all nations,
> baptizing them in the name of the Father and of the
> Son and of the Holy Spirit, teaching them to observe
> all that I have commanded you. And behold, I am
> with you always, to the end of the age."
> —*Matthew 28:18-19 (ESV)*

There is one small word in Matthew's writing that I want to underline and emphasize. How much authority did he say I received? ALL!

And all authority where? In both, heaven and earth.

This is when the Prince of the powers of the air was forced out of his position. This is when he lost control and authority. This is when I claimed authority over all the gentile nations. This is when the gods who once abused their guardianship of the nations lost their positions. And, once again, Paul was a champion of recording what I taught him. He said,

> "and what is the immeasurable greatness of his power toward us who believe, according to the working of his great might that he worked in Christ when he raised him from the dead and seated him at his right hand in the heavenly places, far above all rule and authority and power and dominion, and above every name that is named, not only in this age but also in the one to come."
>
> *—Ephesians 1:19-21 (ESV)*

I've covered a lot in this letter, so let's do a quick review before discovering more.

- I fulfilled all prophecies.
- I fulfilled all the requirements for my earthly ministry.
- I substituted myself for you and died for your sins.
- By doing that, I tempered the anger of God the Father against your sins.
- I triumphed over the fallen angels in prison.
- I brought all powers and authority into captivity.
- And, all power and authority over all in heaven and earth was given to Me.

So, it's all finished? – Sorry, but no. Even though a lot was done, My job is not yet finished, there is still more to be completed.

I know you are familiar with the phrase, but maybe not in the context we're talking about. I told my disciples that I would go and prepare a place for them, and you. And that I would come again and take you to myself, so that where I am you can be there with me (John 14:1-3).

And I made a promise that I would come again. Rest on that. Be assured of that. It is my promise. I am coming again!

It doesn't take a scholar to look at the daily news and quickly realize that the earth is not yet under my Lordship. The gods of the gentile nations have lost the authority that was once theirs, but that doesn't mean they are not still powers to be reckoned with.

Before I ascended back into heaven, I commissioned my followers to take the good news to every tongue, tribe, and nation. I had trained them for three years to be the leaders of a new force on planet earth. I gave gifts of apostles, prophets, evangelists, pastors, and teachers for the completing of the saints (Ephesians 4:11-13).

Yes, I had trained the leaders of a new army, one that would take my *good* news to every people-group on earth. They would encounter people who needed and wanted forgiveness of sin, as well as spiritual beings who have not yet let loose of the human beings they have held captive for so long.

In John's writing of Revelation, he described a scene of throngs of peoples from every nation shouting in exaltation, and worship in another heavenly scene that affirmed all the years of struggle, the battles, and the martyrs was finally worthwhile. Now the work, the authority and my reach would be finished. The work of the apostles I left to carry out is finished and the reach of the church to all nations is finished.

John described the scene so well by saying,

> "And they sang a new song, saying, 'Worthy are you to take the scroll and to open its seals, for you were slain, and by your blood you ransomed people for God from every tribe and language and people and nation, and you have made them a kingdom and priests to our God, and they shall reign on the earth."
>
> —*Revelations 5:9-11 (ESV)*

When that day arrives, I will put all things in order. Chaos will end. Sin will be banished. Evil will have been conquered and vanquished. At that time… "It will all be finished – and a new beginning arrives.

Let me show you what John says it will be like:

> "Then the seventh angel blew his trumpet, and there were loud voices in heaven, saying, 'The kingdom of the world has become the kingdom of our Lord and of his Christ, and he shall reign forever and ever.' And the twenty-four elders who sit on their thrones before God fell on their faces and worshiped God, saying, 'We give thanks to you, Lord God Almighty, who is and who was, for you have taken your great power and begun to reign."
>
> —*Revelations 11:15-17 (ESV)*

Then comes the end, when I deliver the kingdom to God the Father after destroying every rule and every authority and power (1 Corinthians 15:14).

Adam, if you are now thinking of asking, "Is it finished now?" The answer is, "No". This is the new beginning. The world, the creation, the cosmos... all of it has been groaning in travail, waiting for the time when all would be put right. All that is evil, all that is foreign to the command and heart of God will have been justly and aptly put in place and placed in harmony with my original intentions.

This is when my "Jesus box" of goodness is opened and shared with all. It will finally be the way you had always hoped it would be and should be.

Having put all authorities, principalities, and powers under my feet...

Having judged all evil, abhorrent, wicked and opposition...

Having dealt with death and hell...

Having all authority transferred back to me...

And having it all given to the Father...

Then, all is ready.

Everything the Father and I wanted...

All that was intended when the words, "In the beginning" were penned...

And all that was desired when I first uttered, "Let there be..."

Well, let's just say,

"IT FINALLY WAS!"

Then and there, the new beginning begins!

Let everyone say, "Amen, Amen and Amen!"

And Adam, as you now know, until that new beginning begins, "The Battle Rages On..."

Finished, but still working,

—Jesus

18

What Do We Do About Judas?
(Epilogue)

Dear Jesus,

I know our conversation is finished, but I still have a lingering question. Can we just add this one in so I can walk away from this project having a satisfying answer to a very perplexing topic?

What do we do about Judas? After all you've taught me, I still just don't know where he fits into all this. I mean, was he possessed by a demon? Was he just evil? Was he a real disciple or did he just sneak his way into the group?

I really don't even know where to begin to find good answers to this question and not many teachers want to deal with it. So, I was hoping that since I have your attention, I'd try to sneak this one last question in and get some insight.

Lingering and still searching,

—*Adam*

Dear Adam,

There are few names that hold such distaste as the name of one who betrays. Of course, there was Brutus, the betrayer of Julius Caesar who is remembered with the quote, "Et tu Brute?" And, we won't forget the American traitors, Aaron Burr, an American Vice President, and of course, Benedict Arnold.

Yes, at the name of a "traitor," hearers become emotional, with thoughts of revulsion. But, in all of history there is the name of one betrayer that stands far and away above all the others and will likely never be forgotten. His name is linked with the epitome of betrayal and "30 pieces of silver" and you know that name: "Judas" or "Judas Iscariot."

The first mention of Judas is found in Matthew's gospel and it includes a description with his name, "Judas Iscariot, the one who betrayed me. (Matthew 10:2-4). He was going to betray the "anointed one," the "lamb that will take away the sin of the world.

But Judas was just a man. Why include his name in a book about spiritual encounters? Because he is the abject description of some kind of spiritual encounter. As you wade through the following scriptures, I remind you of, you'll be surprised at just how much the written Word has to say about Judas, who he was, and what he did.

Matthew described him as one of the twelve, who went to the chief priests and asked what they would do if he delivered me over to them? And you know what happened, they paid him thirty pieces of silver (Matthew 26:14-15).

Mark tells you of that same moment, but with a little more information, saying that Judas went to the chief priests *in order to betray me to them*. Of course, when they heard what he wanted to do, they were glad and promised to give him money. And then Judas began to seek an opportunity to betray me (Mark 14:10).

And finally, Luke describes the events in his own style, saying Satan entered into Judas, who then went away and conferred with the chief priests and officers how he might betray me (Luke 22:3).

Once you begin to accumulate all the points of view in this story, it begins to paint a disturbing picture. You are probably wondering, "How did Judas, a follower of Christ get to a place of betrayal?" I'll help you with this because there's a lesson that you need to learn... and learn it well.

Not all my lessons were simple messages... Some were difficult and off-putting to many of my listeners and followers. My teaching at Capernaum was different from my other messages. This one was hard for my hearers and it raised quite a ruckus. Let's review John's insights on this event.

> "So Jesus said to them, 'Truly, truly, I say to you, unless you eat the flesh of the Son of Man and drink his blood, you have no life in you. Whoever feeds on my flesh and drinks my blood has eternal life, and I will raise him up on the last day. For my flesh is true food, and my blood is true drink. Whoever feeds on my flesh and drinks my blood abides in me, and I in him. As the living Father sent me, and I live because of the Father, so whoever feeds on me, he also will live because of me. This is the bread that came down from heaven, not like the bread the fathers ate, and died. Whoever feeds on this bread will live forever.' Jesus said these things in the synagogue, as he taught at Capernaum."
>
> *—John 6:53-59 (ESV)*

I know you've read the scriptures before, but it's important to read this part again. This was apparently the "straw that broke the camel's back" for some of my followers. Let's look at some of the reactions of those who listened.

When many of my disciples heard it, they said, "This is a hard saying; who can listen to it?" I knew that even some of my disciples were grumbling about this. I had to ask them point-blank, "Do you take offense at this? I reemphasized that the words that I had spoken to them were spirit and life. And then I pointed out to them all that *there are some of you who do not believe*" (John 6:60-64).

What? Some of my own disciples didn't believe? That's right, and it applied specifically to Judas. I knew from the beginning who those were who didn't believe what I was saying and who it was that would betray me (John 6:64).

You see, I just linked "those who did not believe" and "who it was that would betray me" to Judas. And, then I topped it off with an even more difficult word to them. I told them that no one can come to me unless it is granted by the Father (John 6:65).

Adam, as you read this now, it's probably not a hard saying for you to follow or understand. From your perspective it's just another set of words from me. Important? Yes, but not hard. Yet maybe that's because you are on "this side" of the crucifixion and resurrection. You know the rest of the story... and you've had the history of 2,000 years since it was said to get used to it. But if you were on the "their side" of the crucifixion – it might have been a stumbling block for you too.

The doubters were more than a few... in fact, it was a "lot" of my disciples, not my twelve, that ceased following me because of these pronouncements.

After this many of my disciples turned back and no longer walked with me. So, I turned to the twelve and asked, "Do you want to go away as well?" Simon Peter answered by asking, "Lord, to whom shall we go?" He knew I had the words of eternal life (John 6:66-69).

But then, after seeing how many followers and disciples turned away, I focused my attention on the twelve apostles… and I knew that there was disbelief and betrayal even among them. I didn't keep silent about this. I questioned them, "Did I not choose you, the twelve? And yet *one of you is a devil." I was speaking of Judas* the son of Simon Iscariot, *for he, one of my twelve, was going to betray me* (John 6:70-71).

Earlier, I showed you that Judas would be looking for an opportunity to betray me… and I knew when that moment would arrive. This unholy act would occur at a most holy time.

It was before the Feast of the Passover, when I knew that my hour had come to depart out of this world to the Father. And it was during the supper that the devil had already put it into Judas' heart to betray me (John 13:1-2).

And this is why the story of Judas is included in this book. Here, you have the moment that he is influenced by the evil one. But, if you were Judas, I don't think that you would have noticed anything at all. Judas didn't "see" the devil enter himself. There was no neon sign reading, "It's happening now." There was no contortion of Judas' body, no levitating in the air as these betraying thoughts entered him…

No, Judas had no clue that his thoughts were not his own… someone put them there. This is by far, the most common tactic and scheme of the devils. They plant thoughts into your head that you imagine are their own – and that's why the demonized don't think their ideas are strange. It was the same for the false prophets, when a lying spirit entered their thoughts as they spoke to the Ahab, the king of Israel (1 Kings 22:22-23).

And, it would have been no different from the Egyptian Pharaoh when God hardened his heart. Because he had no idea his thoughts didn't originate within himself, he did not listen to Moses and Aaron (Exodus 9:12).

As I prophesied that someone at the Passover dinner table would betray me... Peter, probably like many of the other disciples, wanted to know who it was that would dare become so traitorous. Peter motioned to me asking if it would be him. Then, John just came out and asked verbally, "Lord, who is going to do this?"

I didn't make a big deal of it, but I told him that the betrayer would be the person to whom I gave a morsel of bread. And that's when I gave it to Judas (John 13:24-26).

Adam, this is the mode of much of the spiritual warfare that plays out around you. It's subtle, it's quiet, it's what you imagine to be your own thoughts.

But it was more than a stray thought that entered, and entertained, the mind of Judas... for Satan, himself entered also. It's little more than a footnote in the tale of the evening. But after Judas had taken the morsel, *Satan entered into him* (John 13:26).

This is the moment Judas went from thinking Satan's thought to being inhabited by him. I not only knew the betrayer was going to be Judas Iscariot, but I had known it for a long time. Even in my prayer time with the Father, I assured the Father that none of the Apostles had been lost... EXCEPT for Judas, whom I called the "son of perdition" (John 17:12).

I chose my words carefully. But that raises the question, "What is perdition?" It's not a common word that enters into your daily conversations. According to a thesaurus, "Perdition" is synonymous with:

Purgatory

Punishment

Abyss

Inferno

Netherworld

Underworld

Hades

When you don't know what the word means… you tend to just ignore it, skip over it or not even think about it. But as you read it, you should loath Judas…

son of purgatory,

son of punishment,

son of the abyss,

son of the inferno,

son of the Netherworld,

son of the Underworld,

son of Hades.

This list certainly awakens in us an awareness that Judas was a much darker soul than just one of the 12 that made a wrong decision. Paul's writings leave an unholy association when comparing this "son of perdition" to another, the anti-Christ:

"Let no one deceive you by any means; for that Day will not come unless the falling away comes first, and the man of sin is revealed, the son of perdition, who opposes and exalts himself above all that is called God."

(2 Thessalonians 2:3-4; NKJV).

Lest, we forget, Judas was more than a betrayer… he absconded with money from the disciples' treasury. He was the treasurer of the group and was known to pilfer money. What was he going to spend it on?

When it was time for the act of betrayal, I spoke to Judas. I didn't let on that I knew what was in his heart. I didn't use striking words, I wasn't harsh, and I wasn't criticizing. I just spoke… and he knew what I meant.

I said to him, "Whatever you are going to do, go and do it quickly." No one else at the table knew what I was talking about. Some of them thought I meant that Judas, being the treasurer, needed to go and pay for the banquet… or maybe that I was encouraging him to give to the poor outside (John 13:27-29).

With Judas absent from the feast, I got down to business with the remaining disciples. They needed to know or at least have a hint of what was to come… for it was coming sooner than any of them anticipated. When Judas left the group, the culmination of my life and ministry on earth was coming to fruition.

After Judas had gone out, I gathered the disciples closer and began to explain what was going to happen. I told them it was time for me to be glorified and for the Father to be glorified in me. I called them 'my children' and told them I would only be with them a little while longer. They would look for me, but where I was going, they could not come (John 13:31-33).

When you next see Judas, he greeted me with a kiss. But this was not a kiss of love or adoration, it was the 'kiss of death'. For with a kiss greeting, Judas treacherously pointed me out to those who had come to arrest me.

Many people have imagined, pondered and questioned why Judas did what he did... and all their guessing is nothing more than earthly psychological pontificating. They missed the point, the only point that is necessary to explain Judas' actions.

During supper,

<u>*the devil had already put it into the heart*</u>
of Judas Iscariot, to betray me (John 13:1-2).

What more explanation is needed? Just look at the Scripture and the answer is obvious. Yes, you can all guess about Judas' state of mind and wonder what he was thinking... or why he wasn't as devoted as the others... but the answer is clear. Satan was using him... and he was willing.

Did Judas know what would happen to me?

Was Judas trying to force me to expose my Messiahship?

These questions don't matter. Something was wrong inside Judas.

He had a heart condition – he had *no heart* for Me.

Some will continue to say it was about the money all along... After all, the entire scenario was played out in the prophetic words of Zechariah, the Old Testament prophet.

> "And I said to them, "If it is good in your sight, give me my wages; but if not, never mind!" So they weighed out *thirty shekels of silver as my wages.*"
> *(Zechariah 11:12-13; LSB)*

And maybe Judas was one of the reasons Paul wrote to Timothy this warning...

> "*For the love of money is a root of all sorts of evils,* and some by aspiring to it have wandered away from the faith and pierced themselves with many griefs."
>
> (1 Timothy 4:10; LSB)

Nonetheless, it was his heart that was wrong. It was wrong about me and it was wrong about the money too. Judas' heart couldn't be disguised. What showed in his heart toward me also showed in his heart toward money. As I've said elsewhere you cannot serve both God and money. You have to choose. When Judas chose not to serve me, he chose to serve money.

There was much evidence to consider...

He stole money from the common treasury.

He objected when a woman honored me with perfume that could have been sold.

He was "lost." I pointed out that none were lost, but Judas.

He was influenced by Satan.

And, Satan entered him.

Psalms 69 gives us a foretelling about the day my earthly body died and what should be the consequence to those who would take part in my torturous death.

> "Reproaches have broken my heart,
> so that I am in despair.
> I looked for pity, but there was none,
> and for comforters, but I found none.
> They gave me poison for food,
> and for my thirst they gave me sour wine to drink.

Let their own table before them become a snare;

and when they are at peace, let it become a trap.

Let their eyes be darkened, so that they cannot see,

and make their loins tremble continually.

Pour out your indignation upon them,

and let your burning anger overtake them.

May their camp be a desolation;

let no one dwell in their tents.

For they persecute him whom you have struck down,

and they recount the pain of those you have wounded.

Add to them punishment upon punishment;

may they have no acquittal from you.

Let them be blotted out of the book of the living;

let them not be enrolled among the righteous."

—*Psalms 69:20-28 (ESV)*

Harsh? Maybe in your judgment, but in the courts of heaven, the Father and I decided it sounded more like "justness" and "justice."

It's been said,

Judas had…

the best pastor

the best leader

the best adviser

the best counselor

Yet, he failed.

It was *his* choice.

Now, let me cap off this treatment of what was going on "in" Judas, with what happened "to" Judas. Luke wrote it down for you to consider, and I'll bet you didn't give it much thought.

"For the Son of Man goes as it has been determined,
but *woe to that man by whom he is betrayed!*"
—*Luke 22:22 (ESV)*

And when Matthew wrote his account of the gospel, he added
his take with these words:

"He said to them, 'It is one of the twelve, one who
is dipping bread into the dish with me. For the Son
of Man goes as it is written of him, but woe to that
man by whom the Son of Man is betrayed! *It would
have been better for that man if he had not been born.*"
—*Mark 14:20-21 (ESV)*

You should learn from this...

Satan has the ability to place thoughts into our minds.

So does God.

We have a choice whether to test or entertain those thoughts.

*And it's one short step from receiving a thought and being entered
into by Satan.*

*Stop for a moment and realize this: Your thoughts might not be
your own, therefore...*

"Bring every thought into the captivity and obedience
of Me."

—*2 Corinthians 10:5*

And a reminder from David,

"Let the words of your mouth and the meditation of
your heart be acceptable in My sight."

—*Psalm 19:14*

Try the spirits... or as John wrote:

> "Do not believe every spirit, but try the spirits whether they are of Me."
>
> —*1 John 4:1*

Adam, I think this will bring our discussion time to a close. You've had a look at the spiritual realm beginning before time began and concluded when time will matter no more. You've seen some of the inner workings of spiritual warfare and how it can affect mankind.

I hope you've learned enough so you can choose how to live your life well... and how you can play a role in propagating the good that the Father and I bring and want to spread throughout all creation.

Allow me to close with what I mentioned to my disciples many years ago because it's still true today and you need to remember it, process it and live with it.

I told them I would not leave them, that I would send the Holy Spirit to guide them into all truth and understanding. So, Adam, I say it to you as well, I will not, not ever leave you.

Staying with you always,

—*Jesus*

Afterword—
Note to the Reader

Dear Reader,

Thank you so much for reading this book. I hope it has brought some reasonable answers to the lingering questions you may have had. On the other hand, it may have opened new questions that are now lingering in your mind and for which you are seeking answers.

With that in mind let me point you to a few helpful resources:

Before I Was Jesus: 25 Secret Identities of Jesus. Look for it on Amazon or Barnes & Noble.

Read almost anything by Dr Michael Heiser, especially, *The Unseen Realm*. It is also available on Amazon.

I also recommend reading Brian Godawa's works, like…

When Giants Were Upon the Earth

Psalm 82

As you might imagine, these are also available on Amazon.

And, remember this…

The same Jesus that promised he would be with Moses was also with Joshua.

The same Jesus that was with Joshua was with David.

The same Jesus that was with David was with the disciples.

The same Jesus that was with the disciples promises that he will also be with you. So, pray as you need... ask for wisdom... abide in him... and remember, life isn't about us - it's about Him.

When life is good—Worship!

When life isn't good—Worship!

Worship isn't about circumstances—it's about who God is.

About the Author

D r. Gerald D Robison has pastored churches on three continents, traveled and trained Bible teachers in over 25 countries, been a popular speaker for Missions and Bible teaching both nationally and internationally, served on the faculty of both, Bible colleges and a seminary, served as an Instructor/ Trainer for Walk Thru the Bible and taught over 300 Missions classes for Perspectives. After being diagnosed with tongue cancer, he has given more of his time to writing.

Want more? Scan the QR code below and gain VIP access to Gerald's latest news, inspiring resources, and exclusive updates!

Other Books by
Dr. Gerald D. Robison

Cat and Dog Theology: Rethinking Your Relationship With Your Master

Cat and Dog Prayer: Rethinking Your Conversations With Your Master

A Dog's Tale: An Allegory on What's Gone Wrong With Missions and Evangelism

A Beginner's Guide To Spiritual Warfare (out of print, but may be found)

Because He Liked It: 101 Glimpses of God's Glory in the Animal Kingdom

Crocs Eat Rocks: Another 101 Glimpses of God's Glory in the Animal Kingdom

Where Did Grandpa Go?: That's What I Want To Know

Where Did Grandma Go?: That's What I Want to Know (coming soon)

30-Seconds That Can Change Your Life: Learning How to Use the Unused Moments in Life

Before I Was Jesus: 25 Secret Identities of Jesus (coming soon)

Your Final Curtain: How Do You Want to Die? (coming soon)

... and watch for more

www.ingramcontent.com/pod-product-compliance
Lightning Source LLC
Chambersburg PA
CBHW071735120626
46550CB00002B/530